BIRTH OF A SHIP

MIGHTY MO

The Biography of the Last Battleship

MIGHTY MO

THE U.S.S. MISSOURI
A BIOGRAPHY of the LAST BATTLESHIP
by Gordon Newell & Vice Admiral Allan E. Smith, USN (Ret.)

BONANZA BOOKS · NEW YORK

517N04880

Copyright © MCMLXIX by Superior Publishing Company.

All rights reserved.

Inquiries should be addressed to:
Bonanza Books,
a division of
Crown Publishers, Inc.,
419 Park Avenue South
New York, New York 10016.

This edition is published by Bonanza Books,
a division of Crown Publishers, Inc.
by arrangement with Superior Publishing Company.

abcdefgh

Manufactured in the United States of America.

To

HARRY S. TRUMAN

Who, as Junior Senator from the State of
Missouri, saw *Mighty Mo* launched and
commissioned; as Commander in Chief
sailed aboard her; and as an American
admired and loved her,

THIS BIOGRAPHY OF THE U.S.S. MISSOURI
is dedicated

About This Book

S THE SUBTITLE indicates, this is the biography of a ship . . . U.S.S. *Missouri* (BB 63) on the fleet list of the United States Navy . . . "Mighty Mo" to the thousands of men who served aboard her through a decade of hot and cold wars, and to millions of Americans who came to view her as the symbol of Victory at Sea.

This book was not written for those who feel that a ship is simply a mechanical contrivance of man, no more worthy of a biography than a bus, a subway train or a jet airplane; it is written for those who believe, as we do, that ships have lives and personalities of their own; that, uniquely among the structures of man, they take on some of the attributes of humanity. Just as no two humans are ever exactly the same, no two ships are duplicates. Though they may be built to identical plans in the same shipyard by the same craftsmen, each will emerge with a personality of its own. And, like men, the noblest and most majestic of ships can fall prey to those slings and arrows of outrageous fortune which so quickly turn the sublime to the ridiculous.

U.S.S. *Missouri* is living evidence of these truths. Four of her class were built during the second World War, to identical plans. The others were completed first and so had a longer time to distinguish themselves in combat. And distinguish themselves they did, yet how many average citizens remember the names of the other three . . . even though one of them, *U.S.S. New Jersey,* is today a unit of our naval forces in Vietnam and the only active battleship in the world?

Having become the center of the whole world's attention when the deadliest conflict in the history of mankind ended upon her quarterdeck; having achieved a public image as the very epitome of the might and majesty of American sea power, *Mighty Mo* blundered upon a well charted shoal in Chesapeake Bay. And there she sat for fifteen days, an acute embarrassment to the United States Navy and the butt of ridicule from the Army Officers' Club at Fortress Monroe, whose windows offered an excellent view of her plight, to the Kremlin in Moscow.

Mighty Mo and the Navy regained their dignity as the result of a salvage operation of a magnitude unequalled since the aftermath of Pearl Harbor, and she hoisted her battle flag again to unleash the terrible power of her broadsides against the Communist Chinese hordes in Korea.

In 1955 *Mighty Mo* joined the inactive fleet at the United States Naval Shipyard, Bremerton, Washington. Thus ended her active career of more than a decade. During much of that period she was the only active battleship on any of the world's oceans. Every year she is visited by thousands of admirers, who stand where MacArthur stood . . . and Jonathan Wainwright and "Bull" Halsey and Nimitz and the other legendary figures of the War in the Pacific.

Like two other United States naval vessels still afloat . . . the frigate *Constitution* and Admiral Dewey's old flagship, light cruiser *Olympia* . . . U.S.S. *Missouri* has become a national shrine and a memorial to a century and a half of American naval history. One other ship, U.S.S. *Arizona,* shares this place of honor, but she is not afloat. Blasted to the bottom of Pearl Harbor on December 7, 1941, she remains a tomb for 1,108 of her officers and men . . . but she is still a commissioned ship of the Navy, her ensign flies over her at full staff, and no other American warship will ever bear her name.

Unlike the others, *Mighty Mo* is still in fighting trim, ready like her sister ship *New Jersey,* to steam again if she is called upon to serve. In this uncertain world new chapters may be added to her biography in years ahead.

This is the story of *Missouri's* first quarter century . . . and of some of the men who have served her and some of the other gallant ships that have served with her.

This is the biography of a ship.

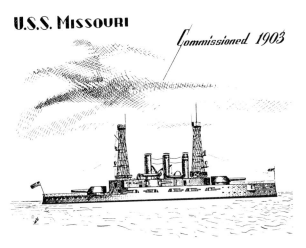

U.S.S. MISSOURI

Commissioned 1903

U.S.S. MISSOURI

Acknowledgements

THE SPECIAL THANKS of the authors is extended to the following individuals who made important contributions to the biography of U.S.S. *Missouri*: Admiral H. P. Smith, Vice Admiral Irving T. Duke, and Vice Admiral William M. Callaghan, former captains of the *Missouri,* who provided first-hand accounts of her exploits; Admiral Arthur D. Struble, commander of the Seventh Fleet during the early naval action in Korean waters, Captain James R. Topper, his Service Force commander, and Vice Admiral Frank Watkins, for additional personal recollections; Vice Admiral Homer N. Wallin, for detailed information on the *Missouri's* refloating following her stranding in Chesapeake Bay; Rear Admiral E. M. Eller, Director of Naval History, and Captain F. Kent Loomis, Assistant Director, who provided the *Missouri's* war diaries and other important source material, and Captain Frank A. Manson of the Directorate for Defense Information, for photographs and historical materials. Very special thanks go to H. W. McCurdy, Ensign, USNR (Ret.), who brought the authors together for this project, to the U.S. Naval Institute and U.S. Naval Academy Alumni Associaion.

PREDECESSOR OF **MIGHTY MO,** the second U.S.S. **MISSOURI,** launched in 1901 and commissioned in 1903, is pictured above. On the opposite page she passes through the Panama Canal in July, 1915, soon after its opening. The old Missouri was extensively rebuilt in 1911, acquiring the "basket masts" which were the trademark of American battleships for many years.

photo courtesy Vice Admiral A. M. Bledsoe

CONTENTS

THE FIRST U.S.S. **MISSOURI** on fire at Gibralter, 1843.
    . . . *The Mariners Museum*

Chapter One

Heritage Of The Past

ON JANUARY 29, 1944, at the New York Naval Shipyard in Brooklyn, a pretty blonde girl named Margaret Truman smashed a beribboned bottle of champagne against a massive steel prow, a naval band struck up the *Missouri Waltz,* favorite of Margaret's father, Senator Harry S. Truman, and the 45,000 displacement tons of the United States Battleship *Missouri* slid ponderously down the ways. The last and greatest of the battleships was afloat. Even before her launching she was a subject of controversy, described by critics as a "hundred million dollar white elephant" . . . a "senile leviathan," already made archaic by air power.

A quarter of a century later, having served the nation in two atom age wars and achieving a status of historical shrine shared only by two or three other United States naval vessels, *Mighty Mo* remains a unit of the fleet, visited by thousands at her quiet mooring in Bremerton, Washington, but ready, like her sister ship, U.S.S. *New Jersey,* to steam and fight again if need be.

Mighty Mo is the third *Missouri* to serve in the United States Navy, but the only one destined to fire a shot in anger. This distinction she shares with a fourth *Missouri,* a shallow-draft river ironclad built in 1863 on the Red River of Louisiana as a unit of the Confederate States' Western Navy.

The first *Missouri,* a side-wheel steam frigate built of wood and powered by a ponderous single-cylinder engine, was launched in 1842, hailed by the American press as the world's most modern warship. The next year, commanded by Captain John Thomas Newton, the *Missouri* left Norfolk Navy Yard with all flags flying and with President John Tyler on the quarterdeck. In Hampton Roads she maneuvered proudly, while the President of the United States watched her twenty-eight-foot paddle wheels drive her through the water at thirteen miles an hour. President Tyler then disembarked at the Old Point Comfort steamboat dock and the *Missouri* headed for the open sea. Her departure was no ordinary one; this voyage, if all went well, would earn her a place in naval history as the first warship to cross the Atlantic Ocean under steam alone. She also carried Diplomat Caleb Cushing, who would attempt to negotiate the first American commercial treaty with the Emperor of China.

On August 18 the *Missouri* put in at Fayal to load stores, water and coal. After departing for the last leg of her trans-Atlantic voyage, Gibralter, the warship steamed through calm seas under warm skies. The crew, having washed the Fayal coal dust from themselves, set about scrubbing their uniforms, which were then hoisted on a line between the main and mizzen tops to dry. The engineers, anxious to make the *Missouri's* record as impressive as possible, kept the furnaces well stoked and cinders belched from the frigate's thirty-foot smokestack. Hot embers set the drying clothing on fire, endangering the ship's rigging.

Fourteen years before, Captain Newton had been in command of the U.S.S. *Fulton I,* fa-

Photo of **MISSOURI** (2). Courtesy Vice Admiral A. M. Bledsoe.

mous as the world's first steam warship. While he was attending a dinner party at Brooklyn Navy Yard, his historic command had caught fire and exploded, a careless gunner having dropped an open lamp in the powder magazine. The subsequent investigation revealed that Captain Newton had posted neither safety regulations nor fire bill, an oversight which had been perpetuated on the *Missouri*. This resulted in some confusion, but the fire aloft was eventually gotten under control and the *Missouri* paddled smartly into the harbor at Gibralter the next evening. There followed a day of ceremonial visits, much firing of salutes and more loading of stores and fuel. Captain Newton left the ship about five p.m. to have dinner with the American consul. Below decks the engineers worked on the engine, badly in need of overhaul after the historic and strenuous dash across the Atlantic.

As it grew darker, the black gang found it difficult to see what they were doing in the murky engine room. Like the erring and long-since fragmented gunner of Captain Newton's earlier command, they decided to take a chance on open lights. As they continued their labors on the six-foot main cylinder, an engine-room storekeeper went to the storeroom just above them in search of a beam scale for weighing coal. In rummaging through the hodgepodge of gear, the storekeeper knocked a heavy wrench off a shelf. It struck a big glass demijohn full of turpentine and shattered it. The turpentine leaked through the floor boards and soaked the felt packing the engineers were trying to make fast around the cylinder and steam chest. The turpentine-soaked felt broke loose and fell on one of the lamps. Within minutes the engine room was in flames. Fire spread through the wooden ship with terrible rapidity. Finally the senior officer aboard ordered the *Missouri* scuttled in a last desperate attempt to prevent the powder magazines from exploding. She was anchored with only about five feet of water under her keel, however, and when she settled onto the bottom most of her blazing upperworks were still above water. Amid a series of tremendous explosions and the crash of falling masts and rigging, the pride of the United States Navy was reduced to a scattered mass of wreckage on the harbor floor.

Only the ship's mascot, a pet bear named Bess, was killed, but Captain Newton never received another promotion nor command of another naval vessel. U.S.S. *Missouri,* the Navy's

pride, had suddenly become the butt of international ridicule . . . a situation which was to repeat itself more than a century later to end the naval career of another highly respected captain.

The second U.S.S. *Missouri* had a longer though less spectacular career. Rated as a first-class battleship at the time of her launching in 1901 at Newport News, she displaced 12,500 tons, was 388 feet long and had a beam of 72 feet, compared to *Mighty Mo's* 45,000 tons, 888-foot length and 108-foot beam. Her two triple-expansion reciprocating engines, fired by 12 Thornycroft boilers, developed 15,845 horsepower and drove her at a speed of about eighteen knots. Like the first *Missouri*, she was a coal-burner. The 180,000-horsepower-geared turbines of today's *Missouri,* powered by oil-fired boilers working at 600 pounds steam pressure, can drive her through the sea at almost twice the speed of her predecessor.

Missouri of 1901 mounted four 12-inch cannon as her primary armament, with sixteen 6-inch and ten smaller guns in addition to two torpedo tubes. *Mighty Mo* carries nine 16-inch guns mounted in three triple turrets, twenty 5-inch guns in ten twin mounts and eighty 40-millimeter antiaircraft cannon in quadruple mounts.

The second *Missouri* was a victim of bad timing. Completed too late for the Spanish-American War, she was out of date by the time the United States entered the first World War, and so she found no opportunity to distinguish herself. In the spring of 1904 she made unhappy headlines, as had the first *Missouri* and as the *Mighty Mo* was destined to do, when a turret explosion killed five of her officers and 29 of her men. In 1907 she went to the aid of victims of the earthquake and fire at Kingston, Jamaica, she was one of the first battleships to pass through the Panama Canal after its opening, and served usefully if unspectacularly as a training ship during the first World War. Decommissioned in 1919, she was scrapped in 1923.

The third of the line, *Mighty Mo,* was to have a career neither as spectacularly brief as the first, nor as humdrum as that of the second. The most terrible war in human history was reaching its crescendo when she took to the water at Brooklyn, and no time was wasted in getting her into action. Less than five months after her launching, on June 11, 1944,

AFTER THE CHRISTENING, Senator Truman looks delighted, his daughter Margaret awed as the huge bulk of the **MISSOURI** slides down the shipyard ways. Rear Admiral Monroe Kelly, commandant of the New York Navy Yard, is at the right.

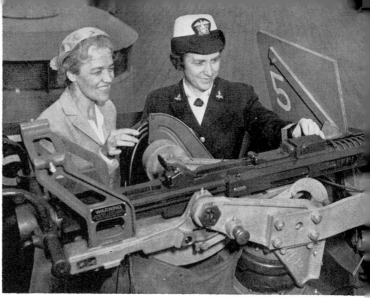

CAPTAIN OF THE QUEEN, W. M. Callaghan, first skipper of the **MISSOURI,** takes the microphone at her commissioning ceremonies to "accept and assume command of United States Ship Missouri". Secretary Forrestal is at the right.

SENATOR MARGARET CHASE SMITH and Chief of Waves Mildred McAfee inspect one of the small calibre units of the antiaircraft armament during a short test firing run off Long Island soon after **MISSOURI'S** commissioning.

LIKE A PAINTED SHIP upon a painted ocean, **MISSOURI** glides through the light chop of the Gulf of Paria, Trinidad, during her shakedown cruise. The camouflage paint, which gave her a psychedelic look, was replaced by an all battle gray color scheme before she sailed for the Pacific war zone.

A GIFT FOR THE PRESIDENT, a scale model of **MIGHTY MO,**
is presented to President Harry S. Truman by Secretary Forrestal.
Vice Admiral Jacobs at the left; Admiral King at the right. . . .
The model is a lasting memento of the proud day when Margaret
Truman christened Mighty Mo.

she was commissioned. Time was of the essence, but that ceremony, marking the transition from inanimate hulk to fighting man-of-war, was not perfunctory.

Captain William M. Callaghan (now a retired vice admiral), had been chosen by the Navy's Bureau of Personnel to command America's newest and most powerful warship. Well over six feet tall and ruggedly handsome, Bill Callaghan looked the wartime motion picture ideal of a battleship captain. Entering the Naval Academy from Oakland, California, in 1915, Midshipman Callaghan made his first training cruise aboard the old battleship *Missouri* of 1901. Graduated in 1918, he had gone on North Sea destroyer duty out of Ireland in the first World War, was promoted to lieutenant junior grade within three months. In 1936 he took his first command, the destroyer *Reuben James*. His last service before taking charge of *Mighty Mo* was at Headquarters, Pacific Fleet on the staff of Admiral Nimitz. More than three thousand naval officers had requested to serve under him aboard *Missouri*.

Enroute to New York via Washington to take over command, Captain Callaghan stopped in at the Bureau of Personnel, where the chief of bureau suggested that he pay a call on Harry S. Truman, junior senator from Missouri, and invite him to make the principal address at the commissioning. Truman said he wouldn't miss the event for anything, but he thought the honor of making the commissioning speech should go to Missouri's senior senator, Bennett Champ Clark. Clark, who as a boy had watched the launching of the earlier *Missouri* four decades before, quickly accepted the invitation.

Early June in New York had been a drab procession of gray and rainy days, but on the morning of *Missouri's* commissioning the sun broke through for the first time, and the day remained beautiful throughout the ceremonies. Then it began to rain again.

Until the day before, only a few key officers and men of her future crew had been aboard. Aside from this cadre, the bulk of the crew had been ordered to the Newport, Rhode Island Naval Training Station for preliminary training and familiarization. On June 10 they boarded a transport and were brought to the shipyard by way of Long Island Sound and the East River. The movement of some three thousand men overland by train or bus would have aroused considerable attention, and at this stage of her career, the Navy wanted as little

publicity as possible about the U.S.S. *Missouri*. By the next afternoon they were ready, in dress blues, to watch their new ship join the Fleet.

At the appointed hour, the ship's executive officer, Commander J. E. Cooper, saluted smartly and told Captain Callaghan, "Captain, I have to report all hands at quarters, sir."

Commander John R. Boslet, senior chaplain, began the Benediction . . . "Almighty God, Ruler of the sky, the earth and the sea, Who are the guide and strength of the men who go down to the sea in ships, we pray that Thou will be present with us who are gathered here to commission to the defense of our beloved nation this mighty ship, "U.S.S. *Missouri*. Grant that in the performance of her stern and somber duties there may be nothing less than the highest fidelity to the best traditions of our Navy and of our Nation."

At the precise moment the commission pennant, the Union Jack and the National Ensign were unfurled, U.S.S. *Missouri* became a unit of the United States Fleet. The first personal flag to climb her signal halliards was that of the Secretary of the Navy. Looking tired and wearing rumpled sports jacket and slacks, Secretary Forrestal had decided at the last moment to attend the ceremony. The Normandy Invasion had begun only a few days before and he, like other top officials at Washington, had gotten little rest. He flew to La Guardia Field and was rushed to the Navy Yard by motorcycle escort in time to add his "Good luck, good hunting and God bless you" to the confident prediction of Senator Clark that "We vision you ultimately leading the way in the subjugation and destruction of the main islands of Japan," and the privately expressed opinion of Senator Truman that *Mighty Mo* was going to "give 'em hell."

Admiral Callaghan still vividly recalls his early days in command of the *Missouri* . . . the thrill of directing a mighty dreadnaught which possessed the grace and speed and agility of a destroyer . . . and the tragedy inevitable in training a green crew to the cruel ways of the sea:

"After a short fitting out period at Bayonne Annex, the ship sailed from New York for the Chesapeake Bay area and the first course of shakedown training under the Fleet Training Command.

"What a sensation it was to have the responsibility and thrill of handling the ship in the open sea after we dropped the pilot at Sandy Hook lightship!

"That first night at sea, however, was marked by a depressing tragedy. During a condition watch necessitated by the submarine menace, a member of a 40-mm gun crew was struck in the chest as the mount was trained too quickly while under remote control. Whether from shock or actual injury to his heart, the crew member died shortly after being rushed to sick bay.

"In the course of transferring his remains via lifeboat as the ship lay to in the entrance to Chesapeake Bay, another near tragedy occurred. The lifeboat was being lowered manually to avoid the possible danger from unfamiliarity with the motor-driven control. As the boat was nearly waterborne, the man controlling the "L"-shaped handle of the forward fall either lost his grip or slipped, with the result that the descending weight of the boat caused the handle to spin and strike him on the head.

Commissioning
BATTLESHIP
U.S.S. MISSOURI

NAVY YARD - NEW YORK
JUNE 11, 1944

"GOOD LUCK, GOOD HUNTING, God bless you and may you come back soon," was the wish of Secretary of the Navy Forrestal (at the microphone) for the **MISSOURI'S** crew during her commissioning ceremonies at New York Naval Shipyard. Harry S. Truman, then junior senator from Missouri, is at Forrestal's left, Bennett Champ Clark, senior senator from Missouri, is at his right.

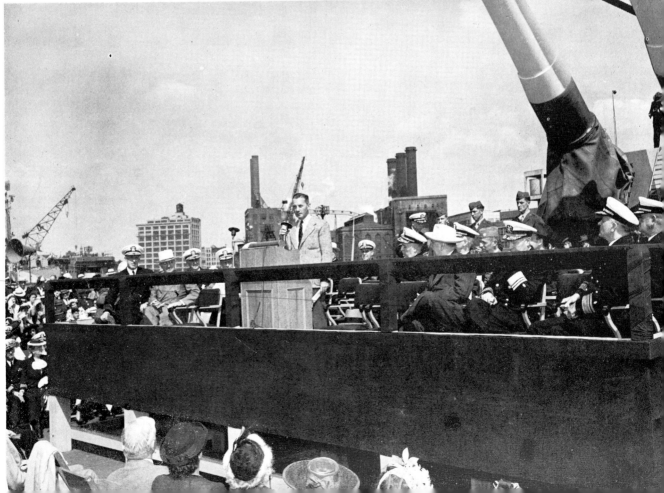

He suffered an almost fatal skull fracture and was in too critical a condition to be moved ashore to a hospital for many weeks after the injury.

"The depressing nature of these two tragic accidents had one immediate beneficial effect . . . it sharpened the awareness of all hands to the fact that we were a raw and untrained group with a long way to go before we could become a disciplined and effective unit of the Fleet."

In the course of her early shakedown activities in Chesapeake Bay, *Mighty Mo* came perilously close to suffering a serious mishap of her own. More than five years later she was destined to appal the Navy and shock the nation by running ignominiously aground in those very waters, and at the very beginning of her career she had a close call. A call so close that even her captain wasn't sure for several anxious hours that she hadn't actually touched bottom and suffered damage in the process.

MIGHTY MO JOINS THE FLEET as her ensign is hoisted for the first time. During the commissioning ceremonies the Colors were hoisted to the gaff on the mainmast because the aircraft crane would have blocked the flag from view if hoisted at the usual position at the stern. Old Glory climbed to the same position when the ship lay at anchor in Tokyo Bay to receive the Japanese surrender emissaries.

The story of *Missouri's* later stranding was told and retold all over the world, but that of her wartime near-miss has never, until now, been made public. Admiral Callaghan has supplied his first-hand account to Admiral Smith for inclusion in this book:

"To the casual observer of a chart, the Chesapeake Bay appears to offer a sufficient expanse of water to accommodate the maneuvers even of a ship of the *Missouri's* size and draft. In the light of the misfortune that you had to agonize over years later as Commander Battleships and Cruisers Atlantic, I sometimes recall with a shudder the episode that could have brought disaster to my career and serious damage to the ship early in her service life.

16

SECRETARY OF THE NAVY James Forrestal is welcomed aboard for the **MISSOURI'S** commissioning by Vice Admiral Fairfax Leary and Captain Callaghan.

lowed to develop I can only add in explanation, but not in defense, that we had started swinging ship in what was plotted as a thoroughly adequate and safe area. The slow ship's speed used, the time required to swing to and steady on each new heading, and the navigator's preoccupation with obtaining readings and azimuths, all served to distract somewhat our attention from the actual ship's plotted position. Lots of water still appeared to be between us and the shoreline, but unfortunately all of it wasn't the depth to float the *Missouri*, even with the modest load of fuel, ammunition and stores we were then carrying.

"That evening when routine soundings were taken it was reported that the forward peak tank indicated two feet of water. Certain that this had been caused by a slight grounding, I sweated through the night until the next morning when the tank was opened for inspection and we discovered the water had backed up from a leaking drain line!

"Preliminary shakedown training in the

"Because of the submarine menace, it was considered desirable if not necessary that all newly-commissioned ships on the east coast, regardless of size, conduct their preliminary shakedown training within the confines of Chesapeake Bay. My efficient and capable navigator had carefully delineated by light solid coloring the limits of all the shallow areas we should stay well clear of during gunnery and other exercises.

"One afternoon, while swinging ship to obtain deviation data for the magnetic compasses, I noticed that we appeared to be being set rather rapidly in the strong ebb tide then running toward a point on the Virginia eastern shoreline. Radar and plot check confirmed the suspicion and, disregarding the navigator's thought that perhaps we should anchor as soon as possible, I rang up emergency full speed and headed the ship into deeper water.

"With what appeared to be almost a humping sensation, the ship responded and we got safely clear of a dangerous situation.

"If you ask how such a situation could be al-

ELDER STATESMAN Bernard Baruch stands in the bows of the **MISSOURI** under the Union Jack (flown only when a ship is anchored or at dock) during a post-commissioning visit at New York. With him is Captain Callaghan.

Chesapeake was followed by further training in the Gulf of Paria in company with the *Guam* under command of Pete Fischler. The deeper water and freedom of the Gulf of Paria was a sweet and welcome relief from the restrictions of Chesapeake Bay."

Although the crew was green and the ship untried, teamwork, communication and quick action had postponed the embarrassing fate which was to overtake *Mighty Mo* in later years. The old adage that a miss is as good as a mile is particularly true in the case of ships and shoals.

After returning to Bayonne for routine post-shakedown overhaul, *Missouri* joined Task Group 27.7 at New York and headed for the Pacific war zone via the Panama Canal and San Francisco. With a beam only two feet narrower than the lock walls at Panama, *Mighty Mo* got through at some cost to her new paint job of battle gray and the loss of a number of scupper lips.

U.S.S. *Missouri*, designated BB 63, had progressed in a few short months from a lifeless steel hulk to a fighting ship of awesome power, manned by a crew skilled in all the manifold tasks of serving the most complex fighting machine ever devised by man. The very ultimate in the development of the modern battleship,

which had begun almost a century before with the ironclads *Monitor* and *Merrimac, Mighty Mo* possessed qualities of speed and maneuverability previously unheard of in ships of such size and armor protection.[1]

On December 24, 1944, *Missouri* entered Pearl Harbor. Three years earlier, the treacherous attack by the Imperial Japanese Navy had left most of the capital ships of the United States Pacific fleet as smoking hulks. Many of them had already been salvaged and returned to service, but the old battleship *Arizona* still lay, as she does today, a tomb for more than a thousand of her company.

As *Mighty Mo* glided past the sunken hulk, still bleeding oil from her mortal wounds, she provided ultimate and dramatic answer to Japan's boast that American sea power in the Pacific had been destroyed.

---

1. Six battleships of this class were a part of the Navy's 1940 building program, *Missouri* being the last of the four actually completed. Another class of five even larger battleships of 58,000 tons was also ordered in 1940, but none were built. These were to have been named *Montana, Ohio, Maine, New Hampshire* and *Louisiana*. Thus the *Missouri, Iowa, New Jersey* and *Wisconsin* were the largest, fastest, most heavily armed . . . and last . . . battleships built by the United States.

ADMIRAL'S LADY. Before a backdrop of **MISSOURI'S** 16-inch gun turrets, Captain Callaghan welcomes Mrs. Chester Nimitz, wife of the United States Navy's Pacific commander, during the ship's stop at San Francisco en route to Pearl Harbor and the western Pacific.

FRESH FROM THE SHIPYARD and gaudy in World War I style dazzle camouflage, U.S.S. **MISSOURI** drops anchor in Chesapeake Bay during initial shakedown exercises.

The Missourian

VOLUME 1   DECEMBER 2, 1944   NUMBER 1

TESTS OVER, MISSOURI JOINS THE FLEET

SKIPPER'S FIRST CRUISE WAS ON OLD MISSOURI

The first cruise that William McCombe Callaghan ever made in the Navy was on the USS Missouri. That was back in 1916.

THE SKIPPER

By now William M. Callaghan has come a long way in the Navy, and he is back on the USS Missouri. He is now Captain Callaghan, USN, Commanding Officer of the newest battle ship of the United States Fleet.

When he made his first Missouri cruise it was as a Naval Academy mid-shipman on the earlier battleship of that name, launched in 1901 and decommissioned in 1919 after serving in World War 1.

Tall (6 feet-four) slender Midshipman Callaghan went to the Naval Academy from Oakland, California, and attended St. Mary's College and the University of San Francisco before entering Annapolis in 1915, aged 18.

Because of the war his class was graduated in three years and in June 1918, Ensign Callaghan immediately went to sea on a destroyer serving on submarine patrol out of Queenstown, Ireland. In three months he was promoted to Lieutenant, junior grade.

After World War 1 his service followed the rotational policy then in effect. In 1936 he was ordered to command the destroyer Reuben James. He went to another destroyer in 1938, and from 1939 to 1942 was in the office of Chief of Naval Operations except for a brief visit to London as a naval observer.

Headquarters, Pacific Fleet, was the next step for Captain Callaghan. He served on the staff of Admiral Nimitz for nearly two years immediately prior to his assignment to duty as skipper of the Navy's largest battlewagon.

45,000 TON BATTLESHIP READY FOR ACTION

The first time most of the ship's company saw the Missouri the huge new battlewagon towered against a dock in the Navy Yard at Brooklyn, in the late spring of 1944, gleaming in fresh war paint.

For more than five years before, the Missouri had been on the drawing boards and on the ways. On January 16, 1941, the keel of this 45,000-ton vessel was laid.

On Saturday, January 29, 1944, the present Missouri of the fleet went down the ways into the East River.

The work of assembling the crew and building the ship's organization soon got under way. Commander William S. Maxwell, who later became chief engineer, handled early details at the Navy Yard and Commander Jacob E. Cooper, designated as executive officer, took charge of the pre-commissioning detail at the Naval Training Center, Newport, R. I.

Something must have leaked out in advance that the Missouri was going to be an outstanding ship. for 3000 officers requested duty aboard her. At Newport the major part of the crew was assembled, sent to various schools and otherwise trained, and soon acquired a reputation as a 4.0 outfit. Meanwhile in New York. Captain Callaghan arrived from the Pacific and took charge.

Then came commissioning day June 11, 1944, on a warm sunny afternoon some 1,500 officers and men came from Newport; the others were already on the scene handling pre-commissioning duties.

Rear Admiral Monroe Kelly, Commandant of the Navy Yard, placed the ship in commission, Captain Callaghan read his orders, accepted delivery of the ship, the order was given "Set the Watch", and for the third time the United States Fleet boasted a U.S.S. Missouri. Since that day the Missouri has been home to more than 2,500 officers and men.

To old hands and new the size and completness of the floating home are a constant wonder. Eight-hun-

(Continued on Page Four)

MIGHTY MO traversing the Panama Canal.
... *photo courtesy Vice Admiral A. M. Bledsoe*

A CLOSE FIT was provided by the Panama Canal locks for the
MIGHTY MO, which had only a foot of clearance on each side.
... *photo courtesy Vice Admiral A. M. Bledsoe*

Chapter Two

Protecting The Fast Carriers

U.S.S. *Missouri* ushered in the first day of January, 1945, by departing Pearl Harbor, bound for Ulithi in the Caroline Islands, where a forward base had been established to support the invasion of Iwo Jima and the carrier-borne air strikes against the Japanese heartland. *Missouri* reached her anchorage at Ulithi on January 26. At midnight of the same day, Admiral Raymond E. Spruance relieved Admiral William F. Halsey and "Bull" Halsey's Third Fleet was redesignated the Fifth Fleet. At the same time, Vice Admiral Marc A. Mitscher relieved Vice Admiral John S. McCain as Commander Fast Carrier Force, Task Force 58. This mighty armada, with eleven fleet aircraft carriers, five escort carriers and eight battleships, was scheduled to begin operations against Japan and in support of the Iwo Jima invasion on February 10. *Missouri* was occupied with provisioning and training operations at Ulithi during the two week lull.

During her stay at the supposedly safe anchorage of Ulithi, the *Missouri's* crew learned something of the dangers of over-confidence during wartime. This haven had been so free from Japanese air attack that the S.O.P. (Standard Operating Procedure) had been modified to permit showing of movies on the open decks of ships at anchor. One evening, with the illuminated silver screens providing perfect aiming points for hostile aircraft, a red alert was flashed. For the *Missouri* it meant only an interrupted Hollywood epic and several hours of Condition I watch at the guns, but for one of the carriers anchored nearby it was a different story. A lone Japanese bomber, sneaking in low and fast, crashed on the carrier's flight deck and exploded in flames.

The resulting fire was brought under control

in an hour or so, but not before lives were lost and considerable damage done to the carrier. It was the first experience of the Fast Carrier Force with the Divine Wind of the Japanese Kamikaze Corps, that elite of death born as a desperation defense against invasion of the home islands. It was not to be its last.

Task Force 58 sortied from Ulithi on the appointed day, and it was reported that "the new battleship *Missouri,* her role in history already shaped by fate and politics, reported for the first time."[1]

During these eventful days, *Mighty Mo* was not only a fighting ship, but a sort of sea-going press box from which newspaper, magazine and radio correspondents observed and reported the action. In the process, they kept things from getting dull for Captain Callaghan and the ship's company when there were no Japanese around to keep them otherwise occupied. The *Missouri's* former commander has a vivid recollection of that episode:

"Someone had conceived the idea (no doubt in Washington) that the impending assault on Iwo Jima lent itself to one of those blow-by-blow accounts by the press and radio media, whose representatives could be accommodated on a large ship near the scene of action . . . a novel concept then for what, by TV standards today, would be a routine performance.

"At any rate, in furtherance of the project, some ten or more press and radio correspondents had been assembled at the Guam headquarters of Fleet Admiral Nimitz and then flown to Ulithi to become the temporary guests of the Ulithi Island commander, Captain "Scrappy" Kessing.

1. **Battle Report; Victory in the Pacific,** Captain Walter Karry, USNR, p. 319.

"Because of her unoccupied flag quarters, the *Missouri* had been designated to receive the gentlemen of the press and to afford them all possible assistance while embarked. As temporary guests of Captain Kessing, their wants had not been treated lightly, nor was their departure from his hospitality lacking in any of the fantastic and unorthodox actions by which his career had been marked. To solace them against what he feared might be hours of boredom awaiting action in the combat area, he had generously provided them with a number of cases of the choicest bourbon and Scotch whiskies.

"The matter came to my attention through the almost breathless report of the executive officer that there was an LCM alongside the starboard accommodation ladder containing our guests-to-be and an accompanying load of cased whiskey already landed on the quarter-deck!

"I directed that the whiskey be turned over to the ship's senior medical officer for storage and safekeeping and that our arriving guests be requested to assemble in my cabin. When so gathered, I informed them in no uncertain terms that shortly after the ship was commissioned I had called all my officers for a conference in the wardroom and, among other strictures I had laid down, was the absolute conformity to the Navy regulations regarding the possession and use of alcoholic beverages aboard ship. Under the circumstances, I could not permit them to enjoy the generous going-away present of Captain Kessing while in the *Missouri,* but that I would insure the return thereof to them upon their departure.

"Much to the amusement of the Exec. and myself, some of our passengers later voluntarily surrendered bottles that had been brought aboard in their suitcases.

"The Iwo Jima battle proved to be a dud as far as proximity for lurid news or broadcasting was concerned. We were too far removed from the bloody action ashore, and on call only for possible bombardment. Our other mission was the usual one of providing fire power protection for the carrier task force of which we were a part."

D-Day at Iwo Jima was February 19, and it was planned that Task Force 58 should keep the Japanese well occupied during the three days before the attack by a continuing series of air strikes over and around Tokyo. These first carrier strikes against the Japanese home islands since the Halsey-Doolittle raid of 1942 were designed not only as a diversionary tactic, but to destroy enemy planes and bases and thus reduce Japan's capability for launching air attacks against the invasion forces off Iwo Jima.

The Fast Carrier Force was divided into five task groups, *Missouri* being assigned to Task Group 58.2 under Rear Admiral R. E. Davison. With her were the carriers *Lexington* and *Hancock,* the escort carrier *San Jacinto,* battleship *Wisconsin,* heavy cruisers *San Francisco* and *Boston* and nineteen destroyers. *Mighty Mo* was still a newcomer to the war zone, her crew untried in combat, but this was not a unique situation in Task Force 58. Aboard the carriers, almost half the air groups were facing their first combat missions.

The full 116-ship fleet passed to the eastward of the Mariana and Bonin Islands, and two days out of Ulithi the air groups were catapulted from the carriers to rehearse with the 3rd Marine Division at Tinian. Two days later the grim armada rendezvoused with fleet tankers to fuel at sea, and the final dash for Japan began.

Far ahead of the great carriers and battle-

D-DAY PLUS TWO at Iwo Jima saw massive naval shelling of Japanese strongholds on Mt. Suribachi.

NAVAL AND AIR BOMBARDMENT creates giant smoke screen at Iwo Jima.

SIXTEEN-INCH SALVOS against Japanese ground troops at Iwo Jima.

ships, Pacific Fleet submarines ranged to destroy any lurking Japanese picket vessels that might give the alarm. Army B-29s and Navy Liberators swept the skies from the Marianas to the coast of Japan. On February 15 a scouting line of five destroyers was sent knifing through the bitterly cold seas and flying scud to screen the carriers. Corsairs and Hellcats screamed from carrier decks to take their antisubmarine patrol positions. At dusk Task Force 58 began its fast run-in toward its launching positions . . . sixty miles off the coast of Honshu and 125 miles southeast of Tokyo. The carriers were at their designated locations by dawn, apparently undetected by the Japanese, thanks to the foul weather as well as the many precautions taken. A strong northeast wind whipped snow and rain squalls across the carrier decks. Broken clouds scudded past at less than a thousand feet and nowhere was the ceiling above 4,000 feet. But Admiral Mitscher had come a long way for what he had predicted would be "the greatest air victory of the war for carrier aviation." From sixteen carriers, the fighter planes roared aloft to blanket the complex of airfields around Tokyo.

Only the planes of Admiral Davison's Task Group 58.2 met major opposition from the Japanese, some hundred Zeros attacking them in rather halfhearted fashion as they were returning to their carriers. Although the suicide pilots of the Kamikaze Corps had already established their tradition of seeking death to strike the enemy, these Japanese pilots seemed far less anxious to meet their ancestors. Despite their reluctance to attack, about forty of them

were shot down. The score might have been better, but American pilots reported temperatures so low that many of the aircraft guns froze up.

The Fast Carrier Group, having brought the bitter fruits of Pearl Harbor to the very gates of the Imperial Palace, turned and raced back toward Iwo Jima to join the pre-invasion bombardment. On D-Day at Iwo Jima, Task Group 58.2 lay 65 miles northwest of the embattled island, while the carriers sent in fighter sweeps. At dusk a flight of Japanese planes, roaring in from the home islands to bomb invasion ships at the beachhead, sighted the *Missouri's* group and made it the target instead. For two hours fifteen enemy planes pressed the attack, while the surface vessels maneuvered behind destroyers' screening smoke and filled the sky with antiaircraft fire. Again, the Japanese pilots seemed less bent on suicide than their brethren of the Kamikaze Corps, and only two direct contacts were made.

The first of these was by the pilot of a twin-engined bomber, who made a determined run at *Mighty Mo.* At 7:53 p.m. he made it to within 9,800 yards of the battleship. There he ran into a wall of fire from her antiaircraft batteries and crashed in flames. U.S.S. *Missouri* had drawn her first blood. Soon afterward another bomber came closer, but was likewise disintegrated by the combined fire of several ships.

On February 23, *Mighty Mo,* with the rest of the Fast Carrier Force, left Iwo Jima, where stubborn land fighting continued, refueled at sea and began another high-speed run for To-

FIFTH FLEET INVASION of Iwo Jima, Mt. Suribachi in the background.

MASSED SHIPS and landing craft of the Iwo Jima invasion fleet are shown in this air view.

kyo Bay. Steaming into the teeth of a northerly gale, even the massive bulk of *Mighty Mo* pitched and rolled, white seas crashing high against her towering prow. Speed was reduced to 16 knots, but the destroyers, required to steam ahead to take their picket stations, caught the full brunt of the storm. A vicious sea struck U.S.S. *Moale,* smashing her bow and opening her forward compartments.

Despite the adverse weather, the carriers launched their first sweeps at dawn on February 25, while still 190 miles southeast of Tokyo. Few of the pilots were able to reach their primary targets, and at noon Admiral Mitscher called off the attack, and headed for Nagoya, where prospects of better weather were reported. Instead, conditions worsened, and speed had to be reduced to 12 knots to avoid further damage to the destroyers. The Japanese home island strikes were called off, the task force refueled at sea, and on March 1 reached a new position sixty miles off Okinawa, destined for invasion exactly one month later.

Although Okinawa was then a center of Japanese air activity, the Imperial forces were again taken by complete surprise, and American carrier planes flew unopposed, bombing and strafing and, more important, taking detailed air photographs of every square foot of Okinawa and its outlying islands. These provided highly accurate charts for the invasion forces to come.

That evening, with the carrier planes recovered, Task Force 58 shaped a southeasterly course and on March 4 entered Ulithi Lagoon to begin routine repairs and replenishment in

preparation for further attacks on Japan and the conquest of Okinawa. During this week of relative tranquility, *Mighty Mo* was transferred from Admiral Davison's Task Group 58.2 to Rear Admiral A. W. Radford's Task Group 58.4. Her fleet-mates now were the carriers *Yorktown, Intrepid, Enterprise* and *Langley,* battleship *Wisconsin,* cruisers *Alaska* and *Guam,* light cruiser *San Diego* and two destroyer squadrons.

On March 16 the Fast Carrier Force was again at sea, headed for Japanese targets in the Kyushu and Inland Sea areas. This time the Japanese air force was better prepared and more in the mood to fight. During the afternoon and night of March 17, radar contact was made with enemy aircraft, but none closed to within range of the ships' guns. At dawn, however, a light bomber swept down on the *Enterprise,* in formation just off *Missouri's* port bow. Crewmen of the *Mighty Mo,* watching the bomb detach itself from the plane and crash down on the carrier's flight deck, braced themselves for the explosion, but it never came. The bomb was a dud. A few minutes later a second enemy plane was caught in a cone of tracer fire from *Missouri* and other ships and exploded into flame. Its pilot kept it on a collision course for the carrier *Intrepid* and it seemed as if nothing could stop him. Although his plane was literally torn apart by the concentrated gunfire of the fleet, it maintained its screaming descent toward the carrier's deck, finally being blasted into the sea so close aboard that burning fragments started a fire on the hangar deck and two of the *Intrepid's* crew were killed, 43 wounded.

BOMBARDING iron and steel works on northern Honshu.

ESCORTING DESTROYERS took the brunt of Pacific typhoons during operations off Japan.
. . . Official U.S. Navy photograph courtesy Vice Admiral A. M. Bledsoe

Early in the afternoon, three more Japanese planes zoomed in on *Yorktown*. Only one succeeded in getting its bomb away, but this struck the carrier's signal bridge, crashed through one deck and exploded, blowing two huge holes in the hull above the waterline and killing or wounding 31 men.

Having fought off these attacks, the Fast Carrier Force on March 19 launched air strikes against Japanese ships on the Inland Sea and moored at Kobe and Kure. Sixteen major vessels, including the mammoth battleship *Yamato* and the carrier *Amagi* were hit and damaged.

The earlier air attacks from the Japanese had been directed against the *Missouri's* group, but it was Admiral Davison's Task Group 58.2 which caught it on March 19. With most of her planes off on strikes, the carrier *Wasp* was bombed by a lone enemy plane which came in undetected. The resulting explosion did major damage to the hangar deck, killed 101 crewmen and wounded 269. By the time the damage was

LINE OF BATTLESHIPS and cruisers steaming toward shore invasion targets on the Japanese home islands.

Admiral Raymond A. Spruance, Commander of the Fifth Fleet.

CRASHING THROUGH TYPHOON-LASHED SEAS, **MIGHTY MO** steams toward her attack position off Japan. This dramatic view from the lower bridge shows her taking green seas over the bow. Number One 16-inch turret has been trained abaft the beam to starboard to prevent its being flooded.

under control she was again under attack by a kamikaze, which missed her by a few feet and exploded alongside. Admiral Davison's flag carrier, *Franklin . . . Big Ben* to her crew . . . was struck by two bombs from another undetected solo plane. The resulting explosions wrapped the carrier in flames from stem to stern, and Admiral Davison advised her skipper, Captain Leslie H. Gehres, to abandon ship. The captain compromised by ordering all but key officers and men to abandon ship. Then, with a skeleton crew, he fought the fires and brought them under control, but the carrier lay dead in the water with a heavy list. Taken under tow, her engineers soon got her own power plant to functioning again, and she ended up making the voyage under her own power to New York for repairs . . . the most heavily damaged carrier in the war at sea to be saved. Her casualties totaled 724 killed, 265 wounded.

No one who lived through the suicidal last-ditch attacks of the kamikazes will ever forget them. The *Missouri's* captain during those harrowing days and nights is no exception:

"Compared to the sophisticated and destructive weapons a ship could be subjected to today, the kamikaze must seem like a bow and arrow relic of a bygone age; nevertheless, it was a fearsome weapon and a hair-raising experience to go through for the uninitiated. Our first was on a beautiful, clear Sunday morning

SPLASH ONE MORE KAMIKAZE as Fast Carrier Force guns converge on would-be suicide pilot off Okinawa.

during the approach for the carrier assault against the Japanese homeland. Alerted by the approach of bogies, the task force had gone into Condition I. Even with this advance warning, two kamikazes came roaring down with the sun behind them and intent on crashing the carrier almost directly ahead of us in the formation. Both were splashed by the concentrated fire of ships in a position to take them under attack. One of the two, however, managed to do some damage to the carrier's flight deck before glancing off and crashing onto the sea.

"It was during this same operation that the carrier *Franklin* was hit and almost lost except for the superhuman efforts of the crew. The ship was not more than 4,000 yards to port of us when attacked, and was soon engulfed in such a mass of flames that we wondered how anyone could survive such an inferno. That the ship did survive became one of the epic achievements of the war."

After the March 19 strikes on the Inland Sea, the Fast Carrier Force retired at reduced speed, sending fighter sweeps back to Japan to keep enemy aircraft on the ground and give as much protection as possible to the crippled *Franklin*. During much of the return voyage to Ulithi, the force was under attack from bombers, kamikazes, and a new Japanese suicide weapon, the 4,700-pound winged bombs called *oka* (Cherry blossom) by the Japanese and *baka* (screwball) by Americans. These devilish devices, carried under a bomber's belly to the point of release, were fitted with jet propulsion and were controlled by human pilots. Once cast loose from its its carrier plane, such a flying bomb was almost impossible to shoot down,

HIT AND SMOKING, but still coming in for this kill, this kamikaze plane was downed just short of a TF 58 carrier.

due to its small size and 600 - mile - an - hour speed. Fortunately, the Japanese didn't have many of them.

Although three carriers were crippled on this foray, no major ships were lost. Vice Admiral Matome Ugaki, commander of the Japanese Fifth Air Fleet, responsible for repelling the carrier attacks, made an effort to "save face" by claiming that his planes had sunk five carriers, two battleships and three cruisers . . . including America's newest battleship, U.S.S. *Missouri*. Admiral Ugaki was so impressed by his own propaganda that he almost convinced the

Imperial High Command that the United States would be in no shape to invade Okinawa for a long time to come. This optimism was to prove costly to the Japanese.[2]

2. After the Japanese Empire, at the behest of Emperor Hirohito, had sued for peace, Admiral Ugaki "atoned" for his failure by leading a flight of 11 naval planes in what was to be the last kamikaze attack against the American forces at Okinawa. He radioed back that he had reached his objective and the planes were diving. But there is no record of any air attacks on American forces in that area, and the complete disappearance of the admiral and his flight remains one of the unsolved mysteries of the war.

LOWER LEVEL WHEEL HOUSE, primary control center of **MISSOURI** during condition watch off Japan. Left to right: captain, officer of the deck, talker.

Chapter Three

Kamikaze!

AS HAD HAPPENED BEFORE, in the Formosa air battle of 1944, the Japanese fell victims of their own propaganda. When on March 23, the Fast Carrier Force began its pre-invasion bombings of Okinawa, the Imperial High Command concluded that it was a mere passing bluff by a hopelessly crippled fleet returning to Ulithi for long-range repairs. Their mistake postponed the planned all-out kamikaze attack on the allied invasion forces until April 6, by which time the landings had already been made. In the meantime, B-29 attacks on the Kyushu air bases crippled Japanese air power. The superforts also mined Shimonoseki Strait, closing that vital supply artery to Japanese surface vessels for a critical week and placing the burden of Okinawa's defense squarely on the shoulders of the 77,000 ground troops of Lieutenant General Mitsuru Ushijima's 32nd Army, with the doubtful support of some 20,000 Okinawan militia and labor battalions.

From March 23 to April 1, Admiral Mitscher kept the Fast Carrier Force at sea some hundred miles east of Okinawa, launching repeated air attacks against that target and its outlying islands. On the first day of its operations in those waters, the Japanese submarine *RO-41* was picked up by sonar. One of the *Missouri* group's screening destroyers, *Haggard*, forced it to the surface with depth charges, then rammed and sank it, the victorious "tin can" then departing at reduced speed for Ulithi and repairs to her broken nose.

The second day, 112 planes were launched from the carriers, intercepting and sinking an entire eight-ship convoy attempting to reinforce the Okinawa garrison. On the same day, March 24, *Mighty Mo,* with her sister ships, *New Jersey* and *Wisconsin,* all of the 1940 class of 45,000-tonners, was dispatched with five destroyers under Rear Admiral L. E. Denfield, to

bombard the southeast coast of Okinawa. For the first time, *Mighty Mo* had occasion to unleash the full thunder of her 16-inch batteries. After this sortie shore bombardment was taken over by the older battleships of Rear Admiral Morton L. Deyo's Task Force 54 and the Fast Carriers returned to air strikes over Kyushu and Okinawa. *Mighty Mo* and her sisters would find nothing bigger than a Japanese bomber to shoot at for the next two months. There were plenty of these, however, for on April 6 the Japanese unleashed their "Operation Ten-Go," the all-out kamikaze attack against the Okinawa invasion forces.

On the same day, the U.S. submarine *Threadfin,* on patrol off the Inland Sea, spotted a Japanese surface fleet steaming southwest at 25 knots. In a final desperation move, the Japanese Navy was throwing its most powerful remaining warship into Operation Ten-Go. This was the mighty super-battleship *Yamato,* screened by the light cruiser *Yahagi* and eight destroyers. This naval version of the kamikaze attack was directed to the Hagushi Roadstead off Okinawa to destroy any survivors of a major air attack planned for April 9. *Yamato* was provided with only enough fuel for the one-way voyage to Okinawa.

Completed in 1941, *Yamato* and her sister ship *Musashi* were the largest battleships ever built. *Musashi's* hulk had lain at the bottom of the Sibuyan Sea six months, sunk by planes of the Fast Carrier Force in October 1944. But *Yamato* had survived the battle off Samar and fought off air pursuit with little damage. Minor damage inflicted by the Inland Sea raids of the carrier force had been repaired, and she remained the most powerful warship on any sea. Her 68,000 deadweight tons dwarfed even *Mighty Mo,* and her main battery of nine 18.1-inch guns could throw projectiles weighing 3,200 pounds, compared to the *Missouri's* 2,-

VICTIM OF KAMIKAZE ATTACK, although brightly illuminated and displaying Red Crosses, was the hospital ship **COMFORT** (AH-6). Some of the damage is pictured here.

southern tip of Kiushu, changed course to west northwest, leaving the lighthouse on the outlying island of Kusakaki Shima well to port in the hope of outflanking the American Fast Carrier Force and coming upon the invasion fleet at Okinawa like wolves among sheep.

Admiral Mitscher had suspected such a maneuver, and by dawn of April 7 his four task groups were at launching positions calculated to intercept the enemy force. At a little after 8 o'clock that morning, a plane from the carrier *Essex* spotted *Yamato* steaming at 22 knots in the center of a diamond-shaped formation of destroyers, the cruiser *Y a h a g a* astern. Word was flashed to Admiral Deyo of the bombardment force off Okinawa, and the battleships of his command moved out to form a wall of steel between the Japanese fleet and the transports of the invasion fleet. But neither the older battleships of Admiral Deyo's force, nor those of the Fast Carrier Force got the opportunity to match their guns, with a maximum

700-pound shells. Quadruple turbines of 150,000 horsepower drove her at a maximum speed of 27.5 knots. Like *Missouri*, she was a singularly beautiful ship despite her tremendous bulk, with a graceful, unbroken shear from bow to stern and streamlined superstructure and battle mast.

But lack of air cover rendered even this colossus of the sea impotent. The Japanese were repeating their fatal error that had led to the destruction of Admiral Kurita's powerful fleet in the Battle for Leyte Gulf. *Yamato* and her supporting warships entered combat without a single Japanese plane overhead to protect them. Every available Japanese aircraft had been expended in the strikes against the Fleet Carrier Force and the amphibious forces at Okinawa. The doomed warships steamed out of the Inland Sea at 10 o'clock on the night of April 6. The crew of *Yamato* had already been assembled and had read to them a message from Japanese 3rd Fleet commander, Vice Admiral J. Ozawa urging them to "render this operation the turning point of the war." The crew sang the national anthem and gave three banzais for the Emperor. Leaving Bungo Strait and the Inland Sea astern, the Japanese warships knifed silently down the Kyushu coast, swung west through Van Diemen Strait, and off the

END OF THE **YAMATO,** the world's most powerful battleship, was signaled by this tower of smoke and flame. U. S. Navy battleships raced to trade broadsides with the Japanese superdreadnaught, but Admiral Mitscher's carrier planes caught her first, with this dramatic result.

range of 42,000 yards, against the huge cannon of *Yamato,* which had a range of 45,000 yards.

Soon after noon the first wave of planes from the Fast Carrier Force roared down on the Japanese fleet through the fire of scores of antiaircraft guns. Two bombs smashed through *Yamato's* deck near the mainmast and a torpedo struck her hull. Destroyer *Hamakaze* took another bomb and torpedo and went down bow first in minutes. The cruise *Yahagi* was bombed and torpedoed and went dead in the water. And the attack had only begun. During the next two hours the remaining Japanese ships were under almost constant attack. Five torpedoes struck the port side of the great battleship *Yamato* during that time. Hundreds of crewmen died when the starboard engine and boiler rooms were counter-flooded to offset the list caused by the portside torpedo hits. The costly maneuver failed, the list increased, and the world's mightiest battleship struggled like a crippled whale, only one propeller working.

Then another wave of carrier planes came in. Torpedoes blew more holes in *Yamato's* port side and nearly a dozen bombs blasted her decks. Only a few light antiaircraft guns remained operable.

At two o'clock still another wave came in to finish off the stricken behemoth. More torpedoes and bombs erupted. *Yamato* circled helplessly, her rudder jammed hard left and listed 35 degrees to port. Twenty minutes later, under a vast pall of black smoke, and amid the roar of bursting bulkheads and exploding magazines, the world's biggest battleship slid beneath the waters of the East China Sea. Only four battered destroyers escaped to Japan; only 269 of the 2,767 officers and men aboard the *Yamato* survived.

The next day the Fast Carrier Force resumed routine support of the Okinawa landings.

Early in the afternoon of April 11 the next massed kamikaze raid began. Strong combat air patrols from the carriers destroyed most of the first flight. By 1:30 p.m. the surface ships received word that thirteen enemy planes had been shot down by the patrolling fighters but that three survivors were approaching the formation at high speed and low altitude. Soon afterward gunners on the *Missouri* sighted a single Japanese "Zeke" streaking for the battleship low off the starboard quarter. Massed tracer streams converged on the kamikaze and it

A kamikaze dives on the **MISSOURI.**

was torn by hit after hit, but the suicide pilot kept his disintegrating plane on a smoking course toward its huge target.

The kamikaze crashed the starboard side of *Mighty Mo* almost amidships about three feet below main deck level. Most of the wreckage, along with the pilot's body, was strewn over the after part of the ship, but one wing hurtled forward to land near the Number Three 5-inch gun mount. Its ruptured fuel tank sprayed burning gasoline over the deck, but the well-trained fire control crews of the *Missouri* had the flames extinguished within three minutes. The kamikaze had sacrificed his life to inflict a few patches of scorched paint on *Mighty Mo.* Later in the day the gun crews drove off a twin engine raider approaching from astern, and near midnight they opened fire on another twin engine attacker which crashed into the sea a minute later. The broken body of the Japanese suicide pilot who had died in vain, was given decent burial at sea from the deck of the *Missouri* next morning.

Not all the ships of the Fast Carrier Force escaped so lightly. The carrier *Enterprise* was struck by two kamimazes which put her out of action for two days. Destroyer *Kidd* was crashed, the plane's bomb passing clear through her hull and killing 38 men. Destroyer *Hale* was shaken up by a near miss while maneuvering to put a surgeon aboard *Kidd.* Another destroyer, *Hank,* took another near miss which killed three of her crew. *Essex* also suffered extensive damage and lost 33 of her crew as the result of a near miss.

Five days later, while still operating with task force 58 in support of the troops on Okinawa, *Mighty Mo,* engaged in the hottest action yet against the desperation attacks of the Kamikaze Corps. From soon after midnight until one o'clock in the afternoon, enemy planes were kept away from the surface ships by their combat air patrol, but at 1:03 p.m. the first formation of kamikazes got through and headed for the warships. Twenty minutes later, *Missouri* opened fire on a low-flying "Zeke" (Zero) headed for the carrier *Intrepid.* It crashed in flames just short of its target. Two minutes later *Mighty Mo's* gunners shifted fire to another plane of the same type. Hit and smoking, it dived toward the battleship and one wingtip actually crashed the ship's aircraft crane on the stern. It was deflected and geysered into the sea close astern, its bomb exploding violently. Wreckage was thrown aboard, and the

. . . and is driven off in flames by her massed Bofors batteries.

Japanese plane attacking **MISSOURI.** Note bomb bursts astern and flak overhead.

These are among the most dramatic photos to come out of the war. The photo below taken moments later from the aircraft carrier, pictures the **MISSOURI** under a black plume of smoke after the suicide pilot's crash.

Kamikaze (left center) zeroes in on **MISSOURI.**

Damage control parties put out fire after Kamikaze strike on **MIGHTY MO.**

great ship shuddered as though she had run aground, but again, damage was slight.

Nine minutes after the first attacker was taken under fire a "Hamp" came screaming in from *Missouri's* port side, its guns chattering. The concentrated 40-millimeter fire of *Mighty Mo* converged upon it, it exploded in flame, swooped low over the ship and crashed into the sea just off the starboard bow. At almost the same time, two more kamikazes bored in on *Intrepid,* one being destroyed by the combined ships' fire, the other crashing into the carrier.

Soon after three o'clock two more kamikazes took aim on *Missouri* and *Intrepid*. The gunners of *Mighty Mo* splashed one well ahead of the carrier and the other close aboard a screening destroyer. Two minutes later a third plane, passing astern of *Missouri,* received the attention of her antiaircraft batteries and was believed downed. During the remainder of the night and next day the enemy aircraft were either destroyed or kept at a respectful distance by the American carrier planes and the ship's 5-inch guns.

The next night the radarmen of the *Missouri* picked up a surface contact which proved to be a lurking Japanese submarine stalking the fleet and looking for an opportunlty to do the most possible damage. Screening destroyers were put on the scent, hunted the submarine down and destroyed it the next morning.

Even the suicide pilots of the Kamikaze Corps grew more wary of the Fast Carrier Force after that, and on April 29 *Mighty Mo* participated in her last kill of an enemy plane, when a hapless "Zeke" blundered in toward dusk and was quickly dispatched by the massed fire of battleships, cruisers and destroyers.

Although the Japanese were obsessed with the need to destroy the aircraft carriers, which bore the brunt of the Divine Wind's blasts, Admiral Callaghan recalls that when the battleship *Missouri* was on station with the Fast Carrier Force, the "threat and actuality of kamikaze attack was almost a daily and nightly matter. It is difficult, unless one has gone through it, to imagine the physical and mental strain of maintaining such a constant state of readiness. Retirement to a rear area for replenishment of fuel, ammunition and food about every five days was a stupendous relief."

On May 6 *Mighty Mo* began preparations for what was to be her greatest moment in history. Detached from the Carrier Force, she proceeded to Ulithi for replenishment and repair. There her first commander, Captain Callaghan, was promoted to Rear Admiral and relieved by Captain S. S. (Sunshine) Murray. On May 17 *Missouri* departed Ulithi, arriving at Apra Harbor, Guam the next day. At 3:27 the same afternoon, amid the traditional ceremony of manning the side, Admiral "Bull" Halsey came aboard. His four star flag climbed the signal halliards, and *Mighty Mo* became flagship, United States Navy Third Fleet.

ARTIFICIAL FOG, shown being generated from the battleship in the foreground, was used to screen the Fast Carrier Force at anchor between raids. **MISSOURI** in the background.

RADAR PLOT in combat operations center.

"16 JULY, 1945; During this period two major British commanders, Vice Admiral RAWLINGS (CTF 37) and Vice Admiral VIAN (CTG 37.1) were aboard with their staffs for a conference with Commander THIRD Fleet. The remainder of the morning and most of the afternoon were passed while units of Task force 38 and Task Force 37 fueled. At 1625, replenishment completed, both task forces set course for an area east of TOKYO from which to send in air strikes and sweeps against the airfields and installations in the TOKYO plains area" . . . *War Diary, U.S.S. MISSOURI, 1945.* Admiral Halsey (in combat jacket with billed cap), Captain Murray (in dark raincoat) and other **MISSOURI** officers and men are shown on the flagship's quarterdeck awaiting the arrival of the British officers.

THE CAPTAIN INSPECTS the **MISSOURI'S** marine detachment.

PILOT'S EYE VIEW of **MIGHTY MO** in fighting trim. Note scouting planes on catapaults at stern.

Chapter Four

At Anchor
In Tokyo Bay

U.S.S. *Missouri,* screened by destroyers *McNair* and *Wedderburn,* arrived back in the front lines of the Pacific sea war on May 26, dropping anchor in Hagushi Anchorage at Okinawa. Soon after her arrival, Admiral Spruance, who had commanded the Fifth Fleet invasion of Okinawa, and Halsey again exchanged commands, the Fifth Fleet being redesignated Third Fleet, and the Fast Carrier Force TF-38. The eighth major kamikaze attack on the ships supporting the Okinawa invasion was launched as command of the fleet changed, with a toll of two destroyers sunk and four transports and merchant vessels damaged. The gunners of the *Missouri* stood to their antiaircraft weapons, but no kamikazes ventured within range of the mighty fleet flagship.

Admiral Halsey had assumed responsibility for continued support of the land forces on Okinawa, which was not yet fully secured, but he did not neglect the Japanese home islands. While Rear Admiral J. J. (Jocko) Clark's Task Group 38.1 continued to plaster the remaining Japanese defenders of Okinawa, Admiral Radford's TG 38.4, with the *Missouri,* spent the first three days of June launching more air attacks against the Kyushu air fields.

Japanese air attacks were few after the kamikaze offensive of late May but in June nature itself unleashed a full-scale blast against the Third Fleet. Weather Central at Guam first plotted the typhoon making up off the Palaus on June 1. Two days later a search plane reported the storm moving north off the Philippines, getting bigger and nastier as it progressed. At this moment, Admiral Clark's ships were rendezvousing with the fleet oilers of Rear Admiral D. B. Beary's supply fleet for refuel-

ing. The following day Radford's group joined that of Clark and the oilers. TG 38.4 now included *Shangri-La,* flagship of Vice Admiral J. S. McCain, commanding the Fast Carriers, as well as Halsey's flagship *Missouri.* The combined fleet steamed on a course of 110 degrees in an effort to clear the approaching storm's track. At this point, its exact location was in doubt, but near midnight the amphibious command ship *Ancon* got a radar bearing on the storm's center. Admiral Halsey received the message at 1:00 a.m. June 5, and ordered a course change to 300 degrees, hoping to cross the storm track and get safely to leeward of it.

Missouri's task group, steaming ahead of and somewhat to the north of TF 38.1, did evade the worst of the typhoon, although the barometer dropped to 29.00, winds gusted to nearly sixty miles an hour, and even *Mighty Mo* made heavy weather of it for a while. TF 38.1 and Admiral Beary's supply vessels caught the full brunt of things. Although only a few miles away, the barometers on Clark's ships dropped to 28.30 as the wind rose to 80 knots, with gusts to a hundred. The destroyers, barely maintaining steerage way at ten knots, rolled an awesome sixty degrees, literally lying on their sides in the trough of the huge seas. Heavy cruiser *Pittsburgh,* steaming at three knots, met monstrous seas, the second of which wrenched off over 100 feet of her bow.[1]

---

1. Next day the fleet tug *Munsee* found the still floating bow section of the *Pittsburgh* and succeeded in towing it to Guam, where it arrived just a day after the rest of the ship. Upon making fast to the unwieldy tow, the skipper of *Munsee* dispatched a message which deserves to take its place with such World War II classics as "Sighted sub; sank same" . . . "Have sighted suburb of *Pittsburgh* and taken it in tow."

Baltimore, a sister ship of the *Pittsburgh*, was sadly wrenched and twisted, but she managed to stay together until she could be gotten into drydock, as did light cruiser *Duluth*, which had her bow smashed upward like a half-opened drawbridge by half a dozen monstrous seas. All four carriers of the task group suffered varying degrees of damage.

Admiral Beary's supply ships took a lambasting too. At four o'clock on the morning of June 5, *Windham Bay* reported winds up to 127 knots, seas 75 feet from trough to crest and barometer at 28.18, with "the ship pitching violently, and the bow alternately plunging deeply with screws racing madly, and then rising to extraordinary heights before plunging again." However, of the 48 ships in Beary's command, only four suffered serious damage.

During the morning of June 5 the fleet passed through the eye of the storm and met relatively calm winds and seas on the other side, but the cost had been heavy. In addition to damaged ships, the force lost 33 planes swept overboard, 36 jettisoned, seven damaged beyond repair and 16 needing major repairs. One officer and five men were killed or lost overboard, and four men seriously injured.[2]

Admiral Radford's group was the only one to come through the typhoon with ships and reputations virtually unscathed, thus adding lustre to *Missouri's* growing reputation as a "lucky ship."

A two-week layup at Leyte put the Fast Carrier Force back in fighting trim, and on July 1 it steamed toward Japan, its officers and men smarting under the criticism of the court of inquiry and anxious to do a bit of face saving of their own . . . at the expense of the enemy. Okinawa was secure at last,[3] and Bull Halsey was free to implement the orders of Fleet Admiral Chester W. Nimitz . . . "To attack Japanese naval and air forces, shipping, shipyards and coastal objectives." Halsey had been itching to deliver mighty blows to the heart of Japan from its home waters, and now his fleet

was in a position to devote full time to that objective. The Fast Carrier Force remained in Japanese waters until war's end.

Course was set for a refueling rendezvous off Iwo Jima, and July 10 air strikes were launched against the Tokyo area. The Japanese air force was hoarding its dwindling supply of planes for the expected all-out invasion of the homeland, and only antiaircraft fire was encountered. The force then retired for another refueling at sea in preparation for strikes against Honshu and Hokkaido, which were beyond B-29 range and had as yet been untouched by the war. Although the force operated within 80 miles of shore, again no Japanese air defense developed to meet the 1,391 sorties flown against Japanese targets.

So far the battleships of the Fast Carrier Force had been assigned the vital but secondary role of guarding the carriers. But at dawn of July 15, Muroran on Hokkaido awoke to the terrifying express train roar of American 16-inch salvos. *Missouri* and *Iowa* had been dispatched under Vice Admiral Louis E. Denfield to blast the steel mills and oil refineries at Muroran, which were pulverized by three hours of bombardment by three of the Navy's mightiest battleships. At the same time, battleships *Massachusetts*, *Indiana* and *South Dakota*, with heavy cruisers *Quincy* and *Chicago*, commanded by Rear Admiral John F. Shafroth, wrought similar havoc on the iron works at Kamaishi. While the battleships and cruisers were thus engaged in the first naval bombardment of Japan, the carrier planes spent a fruitful day destroying the car ferry system which had been used to transport coal between Hokkaido and Honshu.

After again refueling at sea, the Fast Carriers joined forces with the British Carrier Force (TF 37) under Vice Admiral Sir H. B. Rawlings, the combined fleet returning to strike at Tokyo again on July 17. The next day the *Missouri's* group, beefed up by the addition of *North Carolina* and *Alabama*, bombarded major industrial plants at Hitachi, some eighty miles northeast of Tokyo. H.M.S. *King George V* steamed a few miles further north to bombard a suburban industrial plant.

---

2. An eight-day court of inquiry placed heavy blame on Admiral Halsey, with secondary responsibility on Admirals McCain, Clark and Beary. Secretary of the Navy Forrestal was so displeased that he planned to relieve Halsey of command, but was dissuaded on the grounds that it would boost enemy morale. Admiral Halsey, in his reply, stated (with considerable accuracy), that weather warning services were extremely inadequate.

3. Okinawa was taken at the cost of 300 Allied ships lost or damaged, but the Japanese Navy had virtually ceased to exist as a fighting force. Allied carrier air destroyed 2,336 enemy planes, while losing 557 of our own.

For three days beginning July 21, the Fast Carrier Force refueled and took on stores and replacements in one of the largest such operations ever conducted at sea. Admiral Beary's supply ships transferred nearly 400,000 barrels of fuel oil, 6,369 tons of ammunition, 1,635 tons of stores, 99 aircraft and 412 replacement personnel. Then, loaded for bear, the fleet returned for air strikes against the inland sea, which put much of Japan's remaining naval force out of action. The battleships *Hyuga, Ise* and *Haruna* were sunk, along with the cruisers *Tone* and *Aoba*. Carriers *Amagi, Ryuho* and *Katsuragi* were put out of action, as were many smaller naval vessels. As in the past, almost no aerial opposition developed, as the Japanese kept their planes hidden to meet the expected land invasion.

Air strikes, more refueling, and maneuvering to get out of the way of a couple of new typhoons along the Japanese coast occupied the rest of July and early August. On August 7 the Fast Carrier Force commenced a run to strike positions off northern Honshu and Hokkaido, but fog and low visibility prevented flight operations, and the fleet was redirected by Admiral Nimitz to attack a reported concentration of Japanese aircraft on northern Honshu. It was fortunate that he did so, for the Imperial Navy had assembled 200 bombers, planning to crash land them with 2,000 suicide commandos, on the B-29 bases in the Marianas. This dangerous kamikaze nest was virtually wiped out on August 8 and 9, but this time the Japanese air force struck back. On August 8 the combat air patrol fought off Japanese planes, and the following morning the destroyers on picket station came under attack. At a little after four o'clock that afternoon the 40-millimeter gunners of *Mighty Mo* went into action again and a "Grace" was splashed just astern of the flagship and close aboard the carrier *Wasp*.

On this same day, the second atomic bomb, "the Fat Man," was dropped on Nagasaki. Far more powerful than the first, "Little Boy," which had blasted Hiroshimo, it revealed the full and awful potential of the nuclear age.

On the evening of August 10 word reached Admiral Halsey that Japan had agreed to surrender, but her envoys were still haggling over terms. Halsey, whose hatred for the enemy was legendary, determined to keep the pressure on until the surrender became a reality. He proposed to strike the Tokyo area again after refueling on August 11. On that day he invited British Admiral Rawlings to a conference aboard his flagship, and in order to waste no time, H.M.S. *King George V* and U.S.S. *Missouri* lay to port and starboard of fleet oiler *Sabine*. While the two battleships took on fuel, the admirals and their staff officers conferred in the flag cabin of *Mighty Mo*.

Threat of still another typhoon postponed the Tokyo strikes until August 12, when the carriers launched everything they had, claiming 254 grounded Japanese planes destroyed and 149 damaged. Covering fighters of the combat air patrol claimed 18 more in air combat. On August 14 the force refueled and the next morning at 4:15 began to launch the last air strike against Japan.

The next flight was met over Tokyo by 45 Japanese fighters, 26 of which were promptly downed in aerial combat. As the second strike droned toward the target areas, the pilots' headphones crackled with the urgency of the message from *Mighty Mo* . . . "Cease fire! cease fire! The war is over! Cease fire!"[4]

During the mid-forenoon watch, with all planes back on their carriers, Admiral Halsey received final orders to "cease all offensive operations against Japan." Commander Harold E. Stassen, standing the forenoon watch, was logging the day's historic events as they happened:

"0800, steaming as before, position 34-00-00 north latitude 142-11-00 east longitude. 0804 received news flash that President Truman had announced Japan's surrender. 0840 early morning strikes returning and landing as directed. 1055 received orders from Admiral Nimitz to cease offensive operations against Japan, but to continue searches and beware of treachery. 1110 broke out *Missouri's* battle flag and Admiral Halsey's four-star flag and began sounding ship's whistle and siren. All ships in the task force followed the motion. Admirals Halsey and Carney on the bridge to witness the event. 1113 Admiral Halsey ordered the signal "Well Done" hoisted to the Fleet. So closes the watch we have been looking forward to, unconditional surrender of Japan, with Admiral Halsey at sea in command of the greatest com-

---

4. The second strike jettisoned bombs at sea and returned to the carriers, but a six-plane flight from *Yorktown* had barely gotten the word the war was over when it was jumped by 15 or 20 Japanese fighters. In this last major air battle of the war nine of the enemy were shot down, but four of the outnumbered Hellcats were also lost.

bined fighting fleet in all history. As he stands on the bridge I can see a gleam in his eye that is unmistakable."

But even as the deep bass of *Missouri's* whistle reverberated over the sea to signal the end of man's most terrible war, a few Japanese pilots who had not received word of the surrender, or refused to accept it, swept out of the clouds to attack the Fast Carrier Force. They were all shot down or driven off by the fleet's combat air patrol, for there was no relaxation of vigilance on the part of allied naval forces in the Pacific until the formal surrender was signed. Air search, antisubmarine and combat air patrol continued at full strength and ship's companies maintained wartime alert until September 2.

On August 27 the sadly dilapidated Japanese destroyer *Hatsuzakura,* carrying Japanese civilian pilots, moved slowly out of Tokyo Bay and came alongside the *Missouri* off the entrance. On board the battleship the pilots and officials were briefed by Rear Admiral Robert B. Carney, Halsey's chief of staff, as to what was expected of them. He received charts and a plot of the mine fields in the bay. Then *Mighty Mo* raised anchor and moved slowly into Sagami Bay, a few miles south of Tokyo. H.M.S. *Duke of York* steamed just astern of her, followed by most of the Third Fleet. As the mighty fleet swung at its moorings, a red sun dropped behind the snowless cone of Fujiyama, a symbolic setting of the Rising Sun which had triumphed over the United States Pacific Fleet at Pearl Harbor on December 7, 1941.

While aircraft carriers lay offshore to maintain surveillance over Tokyo, minesweepers began the ticklish task of clearing Tokyo Bay. By August 29 the *Missouri,* with other major units of the fleet, had shifted anchorage from Sagami Bay to Tokyo Bay and naval shore parties began to rescue prisoners from the camps ashore. The next morning provisional marine units took over the seacoast forts and the Yokosuka naval base and airfield. Vice Admiral Totsuka formally handed over control of the base to Admiral Carney, while at Atsugi airfield, General Douglas MacArthur stepped from his plane and headed by automobile, with General Eichelberger, for Yokohama along twenty miles of highway lined solidly with Japanese troops, there to protect him from their own die-hard countrymen. At Yokohama, MacArthur set up temporary supreme command headquarters in the customs house, where the final arrangements for the formal surrender were made.

In a fine display of inter-service unity, beefed up by Navy Secretary Forrestal's insistence, MacArthur allowed Admiral Nimitz to choose the surrender site. *Mighty Mo,* named for President Truman's home state, christened by his daughter, and flagship of Admiral Halsey during the final weeks of the war, was his natural choice.

Mighty Mo moved to the mooring designated for her starring role in history . . . a few miles northeast of Commodore Perry's moorage of 1853. In contrast to his tiny squadron of wooden ships, the bay was filled with 258 warships representing every nation which had fought against Japan. Most of the carriers remained offshore to launch a giant fly-over to commemorate V-J Day. From the bridge of the *Missouri,* crusty Bull Halsey sighted a Red Cross-marked hospital complex on shore. "It's probably one of their biggest goddam ammunition dumps," he growled. "We ought to string 'em all up!"

Sunday, September 2, 1945, dawned with scattered clouds that soon disappeared under the sun's rays. *Mighty Mo* was prepared for the ceremonies, a green, baize-covered table set up on the admiral's veranda deck, with the surrender documents in English and Japanese laid out for signing. The flag that had flown over the Capitol in Washington on December 7, 1941, was flying at the main yard. On a bulkhead near the surrender table was displayed the 31-starred flag carried into Tokyo Bay 92 years before by Perry. The light teak decks had been holystoned to gleaming perfection, wartime paint came off the ship's brightwork and brass shone like gold in the sunlight of victory.

Small craft began bringing visitors to the *Missouri* soon after seven o'clock. Fleet Admiral Nimitz came aboard at 8:05, his five-starred flag replacing the four-starred flag of Admiral Halsey at the main. General of the Army Douglas MacArthur came up the gangway from destroyer *Nicholas* at 8:43, to be received by Admirals Nimitz and Halsey amid all the pageantry of sideboys and bos'ns' pipes. At 8:56 the Japanese delegation, brought out by destroyer *Lansdowne,* came up the starboard gangway, headed by Foreign Minister Mamoru Shigemitsu, who had lost a leg in an assassination attempt years before and made his way up

VOLUME 2   SEPTEMBER 10, 1945   NUMBER 12

JAPAN SURRENDERS ABOARD THE USS MISSOURI

MISSOURI'S REPORT OF BATTLE ACTION

Filled with the cream of American manhood, and sprinkled with seasoned veterans, the MISSOURI sailed off to the wars only nine short months ago. Following her illustrious predecessors, she was off to test her mettle against the Japs and take her part in the fighting Navy which was doing so much to finish once and for all Japan's war of aggression The ship was on her way with good advice from her Captain, William M. Callaghan, that the ensuing days and months would not all be spent in fighting but also in many long hours of watchful waiting.

Thus it was not until the nineteenth day of February that the Missouri was destined to see her first action. At this time, while steaming off Iwo Jima as a part of Task Force 58, the ship's first kill was made. At 1944 on that evening several small groups of bogies were picked up by radar and condition one was set in the anti-aircraft battery; as the bogies continued to close "Air Defense" was sounded. Having a good solution on the rapidly closing plane, the ship opened fire and almost immediately the target tentatively identified as a HELEN, burst into flames. This was the first kill for the MISSOURI and one of which all hands could well be proud. Because of good tracking, good shooting, and perhaps a little luck, the reputation of the Missouri spread far and wide as a straight shooting ship.

Not until the eighteenth of March did the ship again have a chance to actually test her shooting ability. This time, still as part of Task Force 58, the first air strikes against the airfields of Kyushu in what was the forerunner of the Okinawa operation. Although bogies were being reported frequently in the vicinity of the Task Group, none closed into visual range until at 0741 when a Jap plane, believed to be a ZEKE, suddenly dove out of the clouds from the direction of the sun and dropped a bomb on the carrier just off the port beam. "Air Defense" was immediately sounded and everyone

(Continued on Page Three)

SHIGEMITSU JAP FOREIGN MINISTER SIGNS PEACE DOCUMENT

When Mr. Mamoru Shigemitsu, Foreign Minister of Japan affixed his signature to the Instrument of Surrender on September 2, 1945 the fighting between Japan and the Allied nations was formally ended. Many precedents were broken in the signing of the

historic document aboard the USS Missouri. Never in all the history of the United States Navy had such an event taken place aboard a ship of war.

On the morning of September 2, Admiral of the Fleet Chester W. Nimitz, USN arrived on board at 0802 with his staff. High ranking Army and Navy Officers began coming aboard shortly after 0800. Generals Stilwell, Krueger, Hodges, Spaatz, Kenney, Doolittle, and Eichelberger were among the Army leaders present for the ceremonies. Perhaps the most noted of all was General Jonathan M. Wainwright, who carried the fight for Corregidor to its bitter conclusion in 1942 and was recently released after three years in a Japanese prisoner of war camp. (Continued on Page Two)

STOICAL IN DEFEAT, the Japanese surrender delegation, led by Foreign Minister Shigemitsu and Army Chief of Staff Umezu, await the victors' orders on the quarterdeck of the **MISSOURI.**

THE FOURTH ESTATE was represented aboard the **MISSOURI** on Surrender Day by both Allied and Japanese correspondents.

SAMURAI SWORDS and dress daggers worn by Japanese peace delegates and attached officers were "checked" in the Flag Cabin of the **MISSOURI** before the surrender document was signed.

the battleship's towering side with some difficulty and in great pain. He was followed by General Yoshijiro Umezu, chief of the army general staff, and three representatives each of the army, navy and foreign office. The civilians wore formal morning attire with high silk hats; the military and naval personnel ill-fitting semi-dress uniforms. Their faces expressionless, the Japanese delegation came aboard between sideboys and accorded the dignity of being "piped aboard." They carried credentials from the Emperor of Japan, which began, "HIROHITO, by the Grace of Heaven, Emperor of Japan, seated on the Throne occupied by the same dynasty changeless through ages eternal, To all to whom these Presents shall come, Greeting!"

The Instrument of Surrender which awaited them on the green baize table was less flowery and more to the point, as the following repro-

INSTRUMENT OF SURRENDER

We, acting by command of and in behalf of the Emperor of Japan, the Japanese Government and the Japanese Imperial General Headquarters, hereby accept the provisions set forth in the declaration issued by the heads of the Governments of the United States, China and Great Britain on 26 July 1945, at Potsdam, and subsequently adhered to by the Union of Soviet Socialist Republics, which four powers are hereafter referred to as the Allied Powers.

We hereby proclaim the unconditional surrender to the Allied Powers of the Japanese Imperial General Headquarters and of all Japanese armed forces and all armed forces under Japanese control wherever situated.

We hereby command all Japanese forces wherever situated and the Japanese people to cease hostilities forthwith, to preserve and save from damage all ships, aircraft, and military and civil property and to comply with all requirements which may be imposed by the Supreme Commander for the Allied Powers or by agencies of the Japanese Government at his direction.

We hereby command the Japanese Imperial General Headquarters to issue at once orders to the Commanders of all Japanese forces and all forces under Japanese control wherever situated to surrender unconditionally themselves and all forces under their control.

We hereby command all civil, military and naval officials to obey and enforce all proclamations, orders and directives deemed by the Supreme Commander for the Allied Powers to be proper to effectuate this surrender and issued by him or under his authority and we direct all such officials to remain at their posts and to continue to perform their non-combatant duties unless specifically relieved by him or under his authority.

We hereby undertake for the Emperor, the Japanese Government and their successors to carry out the provisions of the Potsdam Declaration in good faith, and to issue whatever orders and take whatever action may be required by the Supreme Commander for the Allied Powers or by any other designated representative of the Allied Powers for the purpose of giving effect to that Declaration.

We hereby command the Japanese Imperial Government and the Japanese Imperial General Headquarters at once to liberate all allied prisoners of war and civilian internees now under Japanese control and to provide for their protection, care, maintenance and immediate transportation to places as directed.

The authority of the Emperor and the Japanese Government to rule the state shall be subject to the Supreme Commander for the Allied Powers who will take such steps as he deems proper to effectuate these terms of surrender.

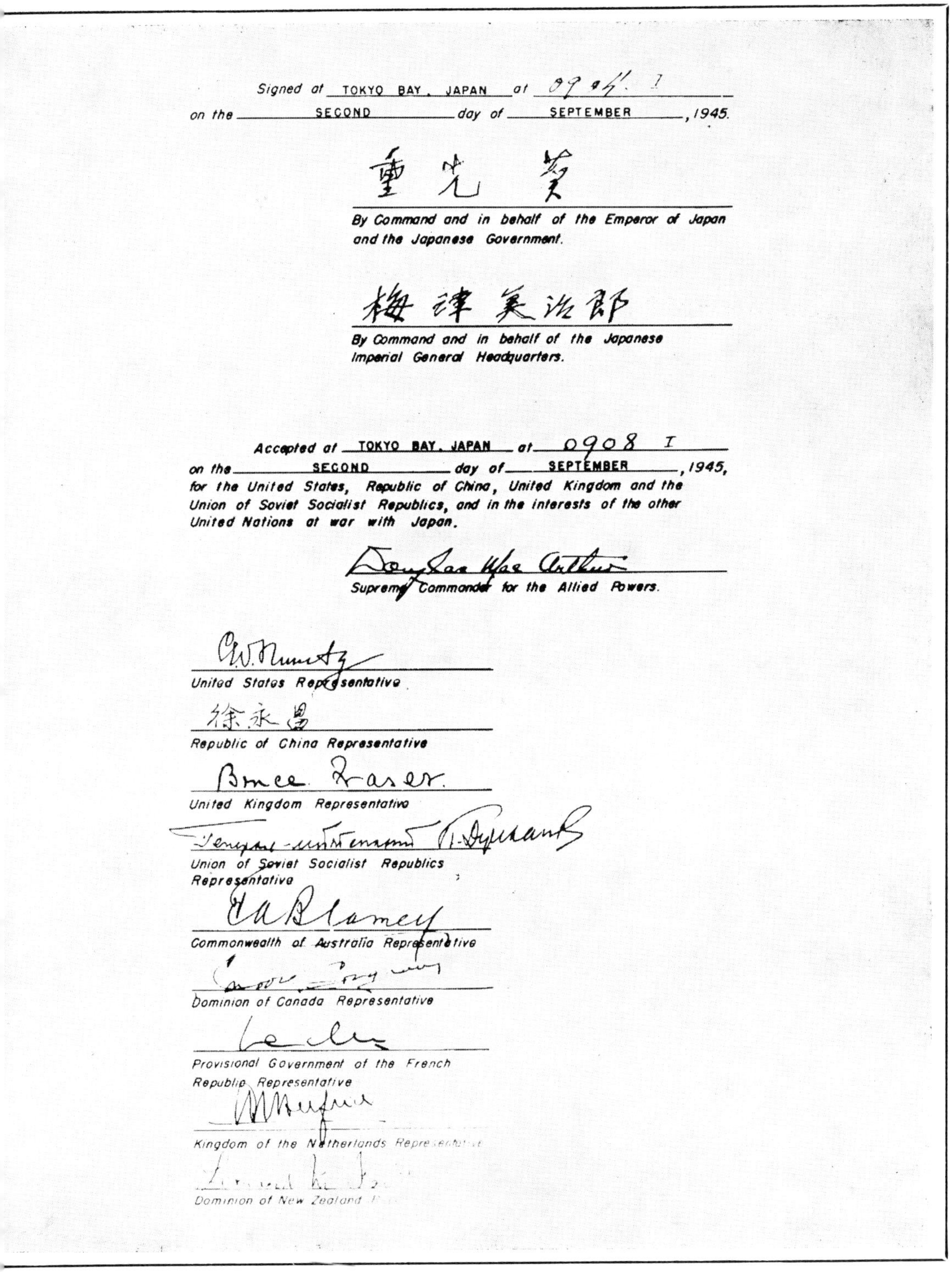

Signed at TOKYO BAY, JAPAN at 0904 I
on the SECOND day of SEPTEMBER, 1945.

重光葵

By Command and in behalf of the Emperor of Japan and the Japanese Government.

梅津美治郎

By Command and in behalf of the Japanese Imperial General Headquarters.

Accepted at TOKYO BAY, JAPAN at 0908 I
on the SECOND day of SEPTEMBER, 1945, for the United States, Republic of China, United Kingdom and the Union of Soviet Socialist Republics, and in the interests of the other United Nations at war with Japan.

Douglas MacArthur

Supreme Commander for the Allied Powers.

C.W. Nimitz

United States Representative

徐永昌

Republic of China Representative

Bruce Fraser.

United Kingdom Representative

Union of Soviet Socialist Republics Representative

T.A. Blamey

Commonwealth of Australia Representative

Dominion of Canada Representative

Provisional Government of the French Republic Representative

Kingdom of the Netherlands Representative

Dominion of New Zealand Re...

duction of the actual document indicates.

The Japanese, representing their nation in the humiliation of its first military defeat, maintained their dignity with Samurai stoicism, but one of the foreign office delegation, Toshikazu Kase, knew the significance of the eleven miniature rising sun flags on *Missouri's* bridge wing, and has recorded that the delegation was "subjected to the torture of the pillory. A million eyes seemed to beat on us with the million shafts of a rattling storm of arrows barbed with fire."[5]

As the Japanese stood stiffly at attention facing the table, the ship's chaplain delivered an invocation over the loud-speaker system. The "Star-Spangled Banner" was then played on a phonograph. Following a brief pause and solemn silence, MacArthur, Nimitz and Halsey

5. **Journey to the Missouri** (1950) p. 7.

SUPREME ALLIED COMMANDER Douglas MacArthur and Fleet Admiral C. W. Nimitz, followed by Admiral Halsey, arrive to start the surrender proceedings. The famous green-covered table is in the foreground. A highly-polished table from H.M.S. **KING GEORGE V** had been brought aboard for the ceremony, but it proved too small and was replaced by the one shown.

arrived from the flag cabin, and MacArthur took his place at the microphones to begin the ceremony. At his side stood the emaciated figures of Lieutenant General Jonathan Wainwright, who had surrendered the Philippines in 1942, and British Lieutenant General Sir Arthur E. Percival, who had surrendered Singapore during the same dark year. Halsey has recorded that "When I spied Skinny Wainwright, I could not trust my voice; I just leaned over the rail and grabbed his hand." Both Wainwright and Percival had last been imprisoned at a small camp at Sian in Manchuria; both resembled walking corpses, their bodies and spirits broken by three years of brutality and deprivation.

MacArthur opened the proceedings with one of the moving speeches for which he was noted, concluding with the hope that "from this solemn occasion a better world shall emerge out of the blood and carnage of the past, a world founded upon faith and understanding, a world dedicated to the dignity of man and the fulfillment of his most cherished wish for freedom, tolerance and justice."

The Supreme Commander's words made Mr. Kase, at least, feel better. He recorded (and later informed Emperor Hirohito) that the general's sentiments transformed the *Missouri's* quarterdeck "into an altar of peace."

Kase's sensibilities came close to receiving a rude shock when MacArthur, having concluded his speech, motioned to the Japanese to come to the table and sign the surrender document.

Shigemitsu, stunned by his nation's disaster and suffering cruelly from his ill-fitting artificial leg, fumbled with his hat, cane and gloves and seemed puzzled as to where he should sign. Bull Halsey, convinced that he was deliberately stalling, was taken by an almost overwhelming urge to "slap him and tell him, 'Sign, damn you! Sign!'"

At that moment, MacArthur's voice sounded crisply in the dead silence, as he ordered his chief of staff, "Sutherland, show him where to sign." General Sutherland did, and the Japanese foreign minister penned the three ideographs of his name upon the surrender document at 9:04. He was followed immediately by General Umeza, who slashed his name upon the paper as though wielding a samurai sword. He would have much preferred hari kari to what he was doing, but the Emperor had asked him to perform the humiliating task, and he had bowed to the Imperial will. The war was officially over after exactly 1,364 days, five hours and 44 minutes.

MacArthur, imbued with a strong sense of history and the dramatic, wrote his name in fragments, using six different pens. The first went to Wainwright, the second to Percival; the next was for West Point, and after that there was one for the National Archives and another for his aide, General Courtney Whitney. The last, a red fountain pen, was for his wife and son. Finishing with a fine flourish, he pocketed the red pen and rose to make way for Admiral Nimitz, who signed for the Navy.

After representatives of Great Britain, China, Australia, Canada, France, The Netherlands, New Zealand and Russia (which had de-

ALLIED MILITARY AND NAVAL POWER is portrayed by the representatives of signatory powers to the Japanese surrender as General MacArthur begins the proceedings.

clared war on Japan in the final weeks of her defeat and proceeded to grab and loot all the territory possible) had affixed their signatures, General MacArthur spoke a final word:

"Let us pray that peace be now restored to the world and that God will preserve it always. These proceedings are now closed."

It was all over by 9:25. As the assembly of dignitaries, Allied and Japanese, prepared to leave the ship, a massed flight of 450 planes from the Fast Carriers, orbiting offshore, roared over the *Missouri* at masthead height and the sun broke out over Fujiyama for the first time that day.[6]

---

6. "Never before in the history of war had there been a more convincing example of the effectiveness of sea power than when a well-armed, highly efficient and undefeated army of over a million men surrendered their homeland unconditionally to the invader without even token resistance." **U. S. Navy at War 1941-1945** Fleet Admiral Ernest J. King, U. S. N., United States Navy Department, 1946.

WITH AN ASSIST from General Sutherland, at his right, and Mr. Kase, at his left, Shigemitsu signs the document that makes official the end of Japanese dreams of conquest.

Missouri remained at anchor in Tokyo Bay for four days; then steamed for Pearl Harbor by way of Guam, arriving on September 20. In less than a year the course of *Mighty Mo* had taken her full circle. She had last entered Pearl Harbor a brand new battleship, her crew untried, her guns never fired in anger. She returned a seasoned veteran, the three battle stars of her Pacific campaigns and the symbols of her kills emblazoned on her bridge. She was credited with shooting down 11 enemy planes and had participated in nine shore bombardments.

And the name of *Mighty Mo* had become a symbol of victory and a household word throughout the world.

USING A HALF DOZEN PENS, General MacArthur signs the surrender document as Supreme Commander of the Allied Powers. Haggard from years of Japanese imprisonment, Generals Wainwright and Percival, flown from Manchuria for the occasion, stand just behind MacArthur.

ADMIRAL OF THE FLEET Nimitz signs for the United States of America.

THESE PROCEEDINGS ARE ENDED, and the Japanese delegation leaves the **MISSOURI**.

ttleship Miss
Vith Halsey Ab
ters Tok.

2 CLOSE CAI

JAPS SURRENDE

TOLEDO BLADE: TUESDAY, AUGUST 14, 1945

Battleship Reported Scene Of Jap Surrender

HIROHITO ORDERS
HOSTILITIES!

ASSIGNS
ARMADA
RRENDER

ON WARSHIP MISSOURI

PRICE TEN CENTS   SPOKANE,

REVIEW   Editorial, Mar

Islands by Acceptan

Propose Battleship
As Surrender Stage.

119 Greater Boston Navy Men
board Battleship Missouri

oard Missouri, Pledges Ju
es Wainwright 'Peace Pen'

TWO YEARS LATER, General MacArthur, at 4th of July parade in 1947, reviews troops of the 1st Cavalry Division in Tokyo. Lt. General Robert Eichelberger, Eighth Army commander, is at MacArthur's left.

. . . U.S. Army Signal Corps photo

51

Chapter Five

"The Great And Wonderful Ship"

WITH WAR'S END and her return to home waters, U.S.S. *Missouri* was assigned to the Atlantic Fleet under a new commander, Captain Roscoe H. Hillenkoetter, who relieved Captain Murray on October 26, 1945. The next day, flying the flag of Admiral James Ingram, commander in chief of the Atlantic Fleet, *Missouri* played host to her old friend and admirer, Harry S. Truman, and New York Governor Thomas E. Dewey during Navy Day ceremonies. Then she moored for three days at New York's Pier 90, where thousands of ordinary citizens came to see the ship on which the war had finally ended.

In March of 1946 the Turkish Ambassador to the United States, Melmet Munir Ertegua, died at Washington. It had long been a common courtesy of maritime nations to assign a warship to convey home the bodies of deceased diplomats of ambassadorial rank. Turkey was proving herself a staunch ally of the Western powers in the post-war realignment and it was deemed advisable to accord the late Turkish ambassador first class attention.

There had never been any doubt in the mind of President Harry S. Truman that U.S.S. *Missouri* was the finest ship afloat. Not only was she named for his home state; she had been christened by his only daughter. Any deluded son of a sea cook who might think there was anything wrong with a ship named *Missouri* and sponsored by Margaret Truman would have the President of the United States to answer to. *Mighty Mo* was duly assigned to convey the remains of the late Ambassador Ertegua to Istanbul.

On March 21 the *Missouri* sailed for Gibralter, where Admiral H. K. Hewitt, commander of U. S. Naval Forces in Europe, hoisted his flag and remained aboard for the rest of the cruise. Escorted by light cruiser *Providence*

and destroyer *Power,* the battleship proceeded to anchorage in the Bosporus off Istanbul, where the body of the ambassador was removed and the ship opened to visitors. This was her first overseas voyage since the end of the war, and it immediately became evident that the fame of *Mighty Mo* wasn't limited to Americans. Awed visitors flocked aboard at Istanbul to view the world's most powerful remaining active battleship and walk the decks where, a few months earlier, the world's bloodiest holocaust had ended. It was much the same at Piraeus, Naples, Tangier and Algiers, where calls of courtesy were made on the return voyage to Gibralter and the United States.

As the other battleships came home from war, they moved, one by one, to layup moorages or to scrapyards. Peace had come and there was great public pressure to get the men of the armed forces out of uniform and to cut military costs. The battleships, those behemoths of the fighting fleet with their huge crews and equally huge operating costs, were most vulnerable. Furthermore, every self-appointed military expert in the country was busily pointing out that the era of the battleship had ended. Air power and the atomic bomb had rendered them as archaic as the sail-powered wooden line-of-battle ships of Nelson's day, and no battleship would ever again serve any useful purpose in modern warfare.

But *Mighty Mo* survived post-war retrenchment. The President saw to it that her bills were paid and the Navy worked hard at finding ways to keep her occupied. In August, 1947, she loomed majestically in the harbor of Rio de Janeiro during the Inter-American Conference on Maintenance of Continental Peace and Security. At its conclusion, President Truman and his official party came aboard, the presidential flag whipped from her main and, to the strains

ASSEMBLY, September 2, 1949, as destroyers and minesweepers join **MIGHTY MO** for the trans-Atlantic voyage to Portsmouth, England.

of the "Missouri Waltz," played on the wardroom piano by the Commander in Chief, *Missouri* glided out of the lovely bay at Rio and returned again to the United States.

Commanded successively by Captains T. B. Hill, R. L. Dennison, J. H. Thach, Jr., and H. P. Smith, *Missouri* maintained a busy schedule of peacetime operations from 1946 through 1949. During the summer of 1948 she made the annual Midshipman Practice Cruise, with Naval Academy and university R.O.T.C. students serving as active members of her crew. At Lisbon, Villefranche and Algiers she again proved that she hadn't lost her charisma, as visitors flocked by the thousands to pay their respects to the mighty ship which had become a legend.

Later in the same year *Missouri* served as flagship, Second Task Fleet, in fleet exercises off Argentia, Newfoundland. There followed several reserve cruises and a major role in the 1949 Atlantic Command Exercises, which included the practice invasion of Vieques Island, Puerto Rico, in March.

Commanded by Capt. H. P. Smith and assigned to Commander of Cruisers, Atlantic Fleet, Rear Admiral Allan E. Smith, *Mighty Mo* was again assigned to lead the 1949 midshipman cruise, this time to England. With five modern destroyers and four fast minelayers, *Missouri* was designated flagship of Task Force 61, commanded by Admiral Smith. On June 4 the training fleet departed Annapolis at dawn and headed down Chesapeake Bay

through thick fog to Norfolk, where 784 first and third classmen from the Naval Academy were embarked. Next day *Mighty Mo* went alongside the naval base dock at high tide and took aboard her quota of the 421 Naval R.O.T.C. midshipmen assigned to the task force.

Highlights of this cruise, recorded by Admiral Smith, make it evident that it was no yachting excursion. The midshipmen were supposed to "learn by doing" and much of their time was spent under simulated battle conditions:

"Taking advantage of the earliest high water, the *Missouri* cast off from the Naval Base dock at 0430, Monday morning, 6 June. With but one glimpse of the channel, the fog closed in again, and we proceeded to sea without again sighting buoys or land until, after passing Cape Henry by radar, the fog gradually faded, and at 10:00 A.M. it became intermittent. The destroyers and light mine layers were directed to proceed independently until clear, and join the *Missouri* later. By noon, Task Force 61 was formed in a circular disposition the *Missouri* in the center and the nine screening ships equally spaced about her at a radius of one mile.

"The first exercise on the schedule was an attack by carrier based planes, which, for the moment, were based at the Naval Air Station, Norfolk. It appeared that the fog would prevent the planes taking off without risk of acci-

dent, but at 1:15 P.M. a flock of planes came in over a low cloud and into the clear opening in which the Task Force was steaming for five minutes, and hit us with complete surprise. Shortly thereafter some torpedo planes came from another direction, low on the water, and were almost as complete a surprise. From this bad start, it behooved me to pull together these friendly ships which were unacquainted with each other and formed in this Task Force for the purpose of accomplishing the results I had stated in my mission.

"We headed north during the night in that same intermittent fog and rain, in order to hold an exercise with our submarines off the New England coast, and also a carrier air group based on Quonset, Rhode Island. Again it appeared that the exercise would be cancelled due to the thick fog and unnecessary risk to ships and personnel in peacetime. However, the sun broke through, and by 9:00 A.M. the visibility was about 5 miles—sufficient to go ahead. We put the *Missouri's* two helicopters in the air, and behind the scouting line proceeded to get our heavy ship past the submarines which were menacing our progress toward Europe. One helicopter sighted a submarine in the mist ahead, about 5 miles in advance of our scouting anti-submarine ships, and immediately hovered just above the periscope— apparently without the submarine's knowledge. One of the destroyers was quickly called to the

scene and succeeded in destroying that submarine. Several submarines were located and periscopes sighted, but one succeeded in getting around our left flank and, at a rather long range, fired a salvo at the *Missouri*. This submarine was undetected up until the time she fired her torpedoes constructively. Then, as scheduled, the submarines came to the surface.

"We then reversed our course for two hours and the carrier air group came in. However, we had been furnished with a combat air patrol, so that this air group had rather a tough time of it before they gained their attack positions and dove on us with their screaming noises. This continued for the remainder of the afternoon, when the submarines again attacked us, and in the late afternoon we settled down into a circular cruising disposition, headed east about Latitude 40, and went into the phase of 'learning by doing.'

"The fog continued nightly for the next four days, but usually cleared about sunrise. At that time daily we would fuel two of the destroyers or fast mine layers from the *Missouri*. The ships, generally, were not up to the standards

GRACEFUL GIANT: U.S.S. **MISSOURI**, center, proves she can turn inside destroyers.

required for fueling, and for that reason this exercise was held more frequently than necessary. The Force would zigzag according to the given plan, and late in the afternoon would form in one long column. The head of the column would change course 90° in order to permit the individual ships to follow around, with the midshipmen responsible for the turning of the ship at exactly the right time in order to follow in the wake of the ship ahead. This requires practice and some knowledge of the movement of a ship in a turn. Between the morning and late afternoon the different type ships were permitted to conduct various exercises within the ships and outside the ships as groups in order to bring their training along. Each day the midshipmen exercised at their Battle Stations so that when the time arrived for Guantanamo, they would be ready to conduct all phases of gun control and firing.

"The helicopters were kept busy in the air acting as targets for the gun control systems, making trips throughout the Task Force with mail and packages, delivery of small spare parts and transfer of personnel.

"For the next ten days the Task Force was busy 'learning by doing' in all departments—Operations, including navigation; gunnery, oc-

casionally using some miniature radio-guided planes as targets; all types of damage control, and the many and varied parts of the engineering department. In all these, the midshipmen, the crew and the officers were intermingled and broken down into small groups to permit the midshipmen to actually perform the operations, under some supervision and security features.

"On Fridays, field days are held and the entire ship is cleaned from stem to stern. The decks are sanded and scrubbed in order to eliminate the oil and paint dropped during the preceding week. The living compartments and messing compartments are all cleaned; then on Friday afternoon an inspection is held of most parts of the ship. In the meantime a Task Force tactical exercise is being conducted which involves maneuvers of various kinds related to situations having to do with offensive and defensive naval warfare. The weather continued cool and with intermittent rains, but gradually cleared as we neared the European shore.

"Two days out from Portsmouth, England, our first port of call, two Royal Air Force planes of the Coastal Command searched for us, located us, and gave the ships tracking drills. During the last night there was consid-

WHERE ARE WE? **MISSOURI** navigator propounds a navigational problem for midshipmen during 1949 training cruise.

FUELING AT SEA. Midshipmen watch as fleet oiler transfers fuel to **MISSOURI'S** tanks while under way in the Atlantic.

erable traffic in the English Channel, a good part of which had the right of way, and many changes of course for the Task Force were made to avoid those ships which had the right of way. This is done by sending over the voice radio telephone circuit a message directing all ships to turn simultaneously upon receipt of "Execute," after they have received instructions as to the movement. The depth of the Channel leading up to His Majesty's Dockyard at Portsmouth is such that the *Missouri* could only approach the Dockyard at high slack water, so we anchored in The Solent, the broader reaches below the narrows.

"The destroyers headed up through the Narrows 5 minutes apart and were moored to the Dockyard piers 3 abreast. It was 7:45 A.M. when the *Missouri* dropped her hook, and 10 minutes later 25 reporters from London and

WE'LL SOON KNOW. Sextant and pelorus are used by midshipmen to determine the ship's exact position.

ADMIRAL SMITH with Admiral of the Fleet Sir Algernon Willis at Nelson's legendary flagship **VICTORY**, Portsmouth.

Portsmouth came aboard for an interview. All the papers of London were represented, and there were several photographers and one or two movie men.

"Ships are commonplace in the everyday life of Portsmouth, or for that matter to the British people in general, and it seemed a little unusual that so much attention should be given to this Task Force. However, the reporters and myself had a very pleasant conference over a cup of coffee, and my staff and myself assisted the reporters in getting the information they desired and also explaining the cruise and the types of midshipmen we had with us. All newspapers had an account of the cruise and most of them had photographs of some of the ships, the officers or midshipmen. The accuracy of these reporters in the accounts which I read was noteworthy.

"At one minutes after 8:00 A.M. the *Mis-*

souri fired a National salute, which was returned by the fort at the entrance to the Narrows. This is an international courtesy rendered by all ships of war on entering a foreign port."

When a foreign fleet comes calling, there are a multitude of ceremonies and affairs of protocol to be enacted. Admiral Smith used one of the *Missouri's* helicopters to drop in, quite literally, on the Lord Mayor of Portsmouth, and the Mayor of Gosport, just across the channel. After toasts in good English sherry to the United States, Great Britain, the Queen and the President, another call was made upon Admiral of the Fleet Sir Algernon U. Willis, RN, Commander in Chief, Portsmouth, where the American commander was piped aboard H.M.S. *Victory*, Admiral Nelson's old flagship, now encased in cement in drydock, but still a commissioned ship of the line in the Royal Navy. Lat-

MISSOURI'S CHOPPER delivers Admiral Smith and staff officers to pay courtesy call on the Lord Mayor of Portsmouth.

BRITISH VISITORS "queue up" at quayside to board **MIGHTY MO** during her stay at Portsmouth.

Lt. Gen. Stratemeyer—Mrs. Stratemeyer—V. Adm. Struble—Mrs. Almond—U.S.S. **MISSOURI,** March 1951.

er there were formal calls on Admiral Richard L. Conolly, U. S. naval commander in Europe, United States Ambassador Douglas and First Sea Lord Bruce Fraser in London. There were formal dinners aboard the flagship for civilian and military dignitaries which, Admiral Smith recorded, proved very successful, although the American naval officers were somewhat embarrassed at the regulations which forbid so much as a glass of beer aboard a U. S. naval vessel. They did their best by having the cooks brew tea for the English guests, but these good intentions led to one of the few criticisms of the American fleet by a British visitor. With horror and incredulity he watched a cook boiling gallons of tea in a huge mess kettle, and later wrote a letter to Admiral Smith, informing him that 'in the British Royal Navy each mess is supplied with several teapots of different sizes, and the tea is made by the good old English method, viz:

"Take a tea pot, lift lid, partly fill with boiling or hot water to heat the pot; remove water. Place several spoonfuls of Indian, Ceylon or China tea in pot, add boiling water to cover tea so as to diffuse it, and after a few minutes, fill the remainder of the pot, internal space, with boiling water. Let it stand for about three minutes and then pour out into cups."

The writer then warned the American admi-

ral that, "with the boiling of tea and water in an urn or cauldron it makes too much tannine and is the cause of stomach or tummy troubles."

Admiral Smith responded by personal letter, as he did to every English adult or child who wrote to him, solemnly assuring the Hampshire gentleman that "I find your suggestions as to the best method of making tea most interesting, and will very soon try them out."

Presumably the flagship's mess cooks had "gotten the word" by the time First Sea Lord Fraser . . . Fraser of North Cape . . . came down from London to revisit the scene of his signing of the Japanese surrender document on behalf of the United Kingdom. There is no record of his suffering "tummy troubles" from American-brewed tea. Lord Fraser, who had gained his title as the result of his defeat of the German pocket battleship *Scharnhorst* off North Cape, "came close to tears as he stood on the Surrender Deck and the emotion of those terrible and trying years and the victory of our arms passed through his mind."

Nor were cultural and scientific ties with England overlooked. A conference was arranged aboard the *Missouri* to discuss two subjects . . . "the Cosmic Ray" and "What is the difference between British youth and American youth?" Four college presidents from Oxford, four from Cambridge, a professor from the

BRITISH SEA LORD Fraser of North Cape inspects the Marine detachment aboard U.S.S. **MISSOURI.**

University of London and the cultural representative from the American Embassy participated with first class (senior) midshipmen and officers of the staff and ship. The visitors arrived at four in the afternoon and so enjoyed themselves that they were invited to stay overnight. The discussions proved so stimulating that the eminent scholars were still arguing when they departed the flagship next day at eleven in the forenoon.

The social activities of Task Force 61 which most endeared its crews to the British were those involving more humble folk, however. On five of the eight days *Mighty Mo* lay at Portsmouth, she was opened to visitors. During the total fifteen-hours of visiting, 32,000 British men, women and children were guests of the *Missouri* and her men. Admiral Smith recalls that, "Many of the men took off their hats as they read the Surrender Plaque, and one could see by their attitude that going through their minds were the six years and more of war which they had endured in defeating the totali-

WELCOME ABOARD is given English war orphans at shipboard children's party during the training fleet's stay at Portsmouth.

tarian states of Germany and Japan. Many of the reactions of these visitors to the Surrender Deck bespoke gratitude."

The crews of all the ships had planned parties for the British children even before the task force left the United States, and the ships' lockers were bulging with toys, balloons, candy and party decorations. England was still in the grip of post-war austerity, and few of her children had ever had their fill of ice cream and cake. Hundreds of them did aboard *Mighty Mo* and the lesser ships of Task Force 61 that summer of 1949 at Portsmouth.

One small girl, Maureen Harding of Fratton Road, Portsmouth, was in the hospital gravely ill, and wrote to Admiral Smith telling him how sorry she was that she wouldn't be coming with her classmates to "visit your great ship." The admiral went to see Maureen himself, and took her gifts with him.

An orphan from the National Children's Home at Southdowns wrote a neat letter of thanks for the "comical films which made us giggle inside," adding that "the tea was a very lovely one. It consisted of cakes, tubs of strawberry ice cream and an apple."

For a few days the grim ships of war which, four years before, had been occupied in tasks of death and destruction, assumed a new significance. Small children came aboard them and had all the ice cream they could eat.

There was an exhibition baseball game at Portsmouth, too, with prizes of candy, cake, souvenir *Missouri* cigarette lighters and tinned hams for the holders of lucky program numbers. Admiral Smith recalls that "one of our

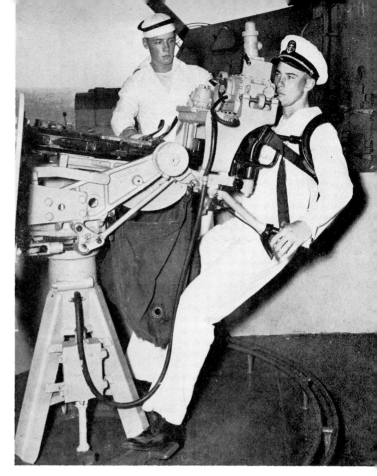

WITH AN EYE ON THE SKY, midshipmen man one of **MISSOURI'S** 20-millimeter antiaircraft guns during Atlantic training cruise.

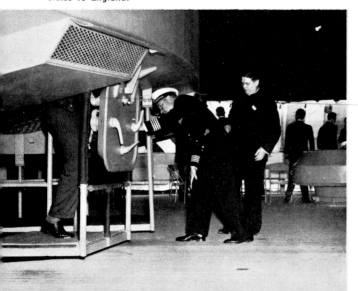

THAT FIRST STEP IS A LITTLE HIGH. Captain Smith takes civilian guests on inspection of 16-inch gun turret during **MISSOURI'S** cruise to England.

officers found a six-year old boy walking around with one of the hams which he had apparently won, and followed him. Presently he caught up with his mother and our officer said, 'I was wondering if anyone was looking after him.' The mother replied, 'Yes, this is the first ham he has ever seen in his life and I have to let him carry it.'

The feelings of the ordinary citizens of Portsmouth were perhaps best summed up in a letter to Admiral Smith from a mother of three who didn't sign her name:

"Dear Sir and Ship's Company:

"First of all, I should like to thank each man in your ships for being so kind to the children. It was a lovely thought on your part to have parties for our orphans. By what I hear and read in the papers they all had a wonderful time. I thank you from the bottom of my heart.

"I do hope and trust the men on your ships had a pleasant stay in Portsmouth.

"I have only seen your ships from a distance, but hope to bring my three kiddies with me on

Friday afternoon, so they will be able to say they have been on *Missouri,* that great and wonderful ship.

"I am only just an ordinary housewife, so I do hope you don't think I have got a cheek writing to you like this. I feel I must thank you for all that you have done for us.

One Portsmouth Housewife"

Her eight-day visit at Portsmouth ended, *Missouri* and her task force set their course for Guantanamo, Cuba, where final gunnery exercises would be held. The return voyage, too, was made largely under simulated war conditions. Admiral Smith's account continues:

"On Saturday at noon the *Missouri* cast off and moved slowly out to the turning circle where she twisted herself with the aid of two tugs and headed down the narrow channel close to the shore. Masses of people blocked the streets which bordered the shoreline, and the sidewalk paralleling the sand beach was covered with cheering crowds. In the soft sunshine the *Missouri* passed between the forts at the Narrows, with one of His Majesty's bands playing 'Auld Lang Syne,' stood down in the Solent and out to sea, heading for the Azores.

"The midshipmen, crews and officers turned to with a will in 'Learning by Doing.' Traffic in the Channel was heavy as usual, but the weather was calm and fairly clear. The destroyers had preceded the *Missouri* by three hours, and, economizing in fuel, we did not join up until the next morning at 8:00 A.M. Reforming into a circular cruising formation, Task Force 61 set its course for the rendezvous with the Navy Tanker *Caloosahatchee.*

"At midnight, in a light fog, the *Caloosahatchee* reported that her radar was not working well, and so near daylight Task Force 61 formed in a short scouting line, and at 5:00 A.M. a 'pip' appeared on the approximate bearing on which we expected the *Caloosahatchee.* When daylight came we had her in sight. Directing the *Caloosahatchee* to take our base course, the destroyers fueled, in order, from *Caloosahatchee's* starboard side, while the *Missouri* eased herself along the tanker's port side. *Missouri* took over 1,000,000 gallons of oil; the destroyers were all down to about 30% of their capacity. The *Missouri* did not cast off from the *Caloosahatchee* until well after dark, and the last destroyer finished about the same time. During the day many midshipmen were transferred to the tanker to watch their fueling operations from that viewpoint, and back again to their own ships. All this was done while steaming along at 10 knots, with only 100 feet between ships, and the possibility of the heavy resultant damage if the massive 50,000 tons of the *Missouri* came in contact with the tanker of 20,000 tons. The moon rose as the fueling was completed, and with all our ships clear of the tanker, I wished the Captain of the *Caloosahatchee* good luck and directed him to carry out his previous instructions to proceed to Portsmouth, England.

"The next morning at 7:00 A.M. we sighted the Azores and passed through the channel between two of the northern islands. While steaming through the channel we sent one helicopter in with air mail to the U. S. Air Force Base. The high peaks of the Azores were continually covered with a mist, and in one of the northern channels there was definitely fog. We continued through the passage, and then set a great circle course for the Antilles.

"By late afternoon the Azores had faded into the eastern horizon and that night we started tactical maneuvers similar to that of the *Bismarck* or *Graf Spee* incident, in which a damaged heavy ship was attacked by a number of lighter ships. Our nine destroyers went on ahead for 100 miles and then, with certain restrictions in order to conserve fuel, they turned once again to the eastward and began to search for the Black *Missouri.* The *Missouri* sighted the enemy destroyers on her radar about 2:30 A.M., and at 3:30 A.M. she had three groups of destroyers, three in each group in the western semi-circle. *Missouri* was limited to 15-knot speed because of our simulated constructive damage, and the destroyers began their attacks. The staff of Commander Task Force 61 were the umpires; the executive officer of each ship was the umpire for his ship. There were special Umpire Circuits set up so that almost instantaneous information of the calibre and number of shots fired were known by the umpires and damage assessed accordingly. The ships were required to repair this constructive damage and reduce their speed or put out of commission the guns or communication systems or other damage awarded. Although the *Missouri* had only half of her ammunition allowance, it soon became clear that the destroyers could not get in on her, and in the course of the next forty-five minutes the *Missouri* 'sank' five of the destroyers and damaged two others.

It was an unequal contest and came out just the reverse of both the *Bismarck* fight and *Graf Spee* fight. When daylight came, about a quarter to five, the engagement was over and a cruising disposition was again formed. The exercises, drills and lectures scheduled in the routine order of the day were then carried out. The tactical situation brought out the advantages and disadvantages of Interior and Exterior Lines—whether one is fighting on the sea, in the air or on the ground. There are many examples of Interior-Exterior Lines, both in tactics and strategy, and especially in land warfare. These tactical situations provide a method for examination of the principles of war, and permit the student of war to back up his thoughts in the same manner as the law student, who analyses his case first and then derives the general rule of law. After that, the law student starts looking at the exceptions. It is the same way in the study of war.

"For the next four days, each afternoon from 3:30 to 4:30, the Task Force stopped and all hands enjoyed a swim in the world's second largest outdoor swimming pool—2000 miles from Europe, 1000 miles from United States, and 12,000 feet from land (the depth of the water was 2000 fathoms). All safety precautions were taken, including riflemen in case sharks appeared; floats, life belts and life boats in the water, and control from the ship by loudspeakers. Cargo nets over the *Missouri's* side furnished the means of getting back aboard after a 15-minute swim. Most of the swimmers found it a tiring task to climb the 30 feet to the deck. It was a wonderful experience in the clear blue water of mid-Atlantic, in which you can see down 100 feet easily. They were refreshing swims in the increasing high temperature of the southern climes we were approaching.

"Late on Thursday afternoon, 7 July, we steamed through Caicos Passage, with Mayaguana Island, Caicos Islands and Great Inaguia Island to the east and west, and the next morning, passing the most easterly tip of Cuba, we changed course westward toward Guantanamo Bay. One of the helicopters went on ahead and brought out Rear Admiral Phillips, Commander of the Guantanamo Bay Area, for breakfast, and we completed all arrangements necessary for the many activities with which we were to be engaged during our stay in this area. There were various types of gunnery practices, anti-aircraft, surface, and submarine exercises, in which midshipmen would embark in submarines and the destroyers would attempt to locate the subs; track and attack them. For weekends, certain recreation and athletic facilities would be needed. The next ten days were very lively and full of concentrated training and activities of the type mentioned.

"Then, on Wednesday evening, 20 July, once more we joined up and started cruising on a course North, up through Windward Passage, and then headed toward Jacksonville, Florida. Two days later, fifty miles off shore, several jet planes came out and attacked us for a good part of the morning. The following day we had an exercise off Charleston with several different types of mines—Aerial Mining by planes from Norfolk, Submarine Mining by Submarine Force craft, and Surface Mining by our own four light mine layers; then there were mine sweepers which came out of Charleston and began sweeping the fields. Midshipmen were spread around and shifted from one ship to another in order to observe and participate in all these types of mining and mine sweeping exercises, which were arranged by Rear Admiral B. H. Hanlon, commander of the Mine Force and former commander of American underwater demolition teams in World War II.

"As the sun was setting we left this area, and the next day being Sunday we released the midshipmen from their watches and gave them a day to prepare to disembark. Rounding Hatteras in the early dark hours of Monday, and shortly after daylight, we were attacked by carrier aircraft from the Norfolk area several times. About 10:00 A.M., with the last air exercise over, we headed toward the Capes, and by 12:30 the *Missouri* was lying off the buoy, preparing to proceed into the dock at the Naval Base. The destroyers had preceded the *Missouri* and were already alongside."

A week later, *Missouri* and her consorts embarked another 1,200 midshipmen and began the second phase of the 1949 training cruise, this time to France. The fourth anniversary of the signing of the Japanese surrender, September 2, 1949, found *Mighty Mo* on the high seas. Officers, midshipmen and crew were assembled for ceremonies on the Surrender Deck commemorating that historic day.

Admiral Smith had dispatched the following wire to General of the Army Douglas MacArthur in Tokyo:

"Today the second of September in the *Missouri* flagship of the Midshipman Cruise 1949

FOUR YEARS AFTER the signing of the Japanese surrender, officers, midshipmen and crew assemble around the plaque on **MISSOURI'S** quarterdeck to hear message from General MacArthur.

we are commemorating the fourth anniversary of the surrender of Japan x The officers and men of *Missouri* as well as the 1200 midshipmen on the cruise who are being trained as the future naval leaders remember your great leadership which is being projected in the future through them unquote x *Missouri* at 020908Q was bearing 100 degrees 258 miles from San Salvador where Columbus made his first sighting of the Americas x A hurricane is forming to the southeastward x"

Never one to be outdone in literary composition as in battle, MacArthur signalled *Mighty Mo* as follows:

"Following in reply to your 020908Z x No message I have ever received either in success or adversity has moved me quite as deeply as your signal x Hurricane indeed may come and go but our beloved country brought to life by the sailor Columbus will weather any storm as long as our own sailors such as are now gathered on the *Missouri* continue to exist x May God protect and preserve them is my prayer from Tokyo as the world keeps turning over and over x MacArthur."

Contre-Amiral ALLAN E. SMITH, U. S. N.
Commandant de la Croisiere des Aspirants
de Marine 1949
Commandant de la Force Speciale, 61

Capitaine de Vaisseau W. K. MENDENHALL, Jr., U. S. N.
Chef d'Etat-Major

U. S. S. MISSOURI, Navire - Amiral
Capitaine de Vaisseau H. P. SMITH, Commandant

IDYLLIC SETTING. **MIGHTY MO** lies peacefully in the charming harbor of Villefranche during 1948 Midshipman Training Cruise to France.

NAVIGATIONAL AID to **MISSOURI** midshipmen in Paris is provided by a friendly native.

CAKE FOR THE CAPTAINS. SD3 Ernesto Galito, ship's baker, produced this masterpiece of culinary art for the 1949 change of command ceremonies, as Captain H. P. Smith took over the **MISSOURI** from Captain J. H. Thach.

MEMORY OF WARS PAST. **MISSOURI** sailors visit the tomb of
Marshall Foch, supreme allied commander in World War I.

Chapter Six

"U.S.S. Missouri
Has Gone
Half A Mile Inland"

BY THE CLOSING MONTHS OF 1949 U.S.S. *Missouri*, last of the United States Navy's battleships to be built, was also the only one remaining in commission. Numerous politicians, and high ranking officers of the Army and Air Force, scratching for scarce post-war defense funds, were vociferous in their belief that she was one too many. Conceding that *Mighty Mo* had earned a place in the hearts of all freedom-loving people as the symbol of victory in World War II, they argued that her annual operating cost of nearly seven million dollars was a high price for maintaining a national monument. The nuclear age was here, and some critics doubted there was a place in it for any kind of surface naval craft, let alone that vast and vulnerable anachronism, the battleship.

Navy men argued that *Mighty Mo* was no ordinary battleship. In spite of her 45,000 tons of sheer bulk, she could steam as fast as any cruiser and could actually turn inside a destroyer. Her sixteen-inch batteries could deliver all the punch of an aircraft carrier's planes and keep on delivering it without pause and with an accuracy never approached by aerial bombardment.

In October, 1949, *Mighty Mo* steamed serenely through this sea of controversy to Norfolk Navy Yard, where she was scheduled for the three months' extensive overhaul given every three years to major ships of the Navy in peacetime. As shipyard workers swarmed aboard, a third of her ship's company, some six hundred men, departed for long-awaited thirty-day leaves. Others were ordered to various naval technical schools for advanced or refresher courses in radar, electronics, gunnery and engineering.

The remaining officers and crew were expected to hold such drills and training as were practicable, but this was easier said than done. The usually spotless decks of the *Missouri* were littered with tools and gear, while hundreds of civilian workers scurried about making alterations, removing old equipment and installing new, and opening and examining all the machinery and mechanical devices aboard the huge and complex ship.

In the midst of the confusion, a new skipper, Captain William D. Brown, came aboard to relieve Captain Page Smith. Tall, slender, tanned and graying, Captain Brown was at the age of 47, a veteran of nearly thirty years naval service, an Annapolis graduate and one of the Navy's senior captains. He had a distinguished war record as a submariner and destroyer commander, but he had never commanded a big ship, nor any ship at all for the past six years. His last service had been in Florida, where he was engaged in highly scientific oceanographic experiments.

A net of circumstances was already forming about the battleship *Missouri* which would soon make her the victim of the most widely publicized shipwreck since the sinking of the *Titanic*.

Captain Brown took command of the *Missouri* on December 10. The overhaul of the battleship's main engines was completed the week before Christmas. On December 23 the new captain took her out to sea for the first time . . . a brief test run off the Virginia capes . . . and brought her back on Christmas Eve. Her next sortie was scheduled for the morning of January 17, 1950, when she would sail for maneuvers off Guantanamo Naval Base in Cuba.

Seamen have always had a dread of Fridays

which fall on the 13th of the month. Mutinies have resulted from orders to sail on that unlucky date, and it was on Friday, January 13, 1950, that the story of *Mighty Mo's* colossal bad luck really began. On that day, Captain Brown received a manila envelope which had come to the ship from Naval Base headquarters and was delivered to him by the officer of the deck. The envelope contained a mimeographed form letter from the Naval Ordnance Laboratory. The letter requested that, in the interest of a scientific experiment, the *Missouri* run an "acoustical range" just to seaward of Old Point Comfort, across Hampton Roads from Norfolk.

An acoustical range operates somewhat like an "electric eye," the gadget which automatically opens garage doors. The chief instruments involved in the Hampton Roads installation were a secret underwater sound device and recording equipment on shore. When ships ran the range correctly, the underwater "ears" relayed to the recorders information about the type of vessel and its exact course.

The captain, harassed by the thousand and one details of getting a new command cleared of dockyard confusion and ready for an extended cruise, gave the letter brief attention. He entirely skipped a paragraph stating that compliance was "optional," an oversight which he later testified was "much to my regret." He didn't even glance at the other papers in the envelope . . . specific instructions for running the range and a description of the buoys which marked it. Instead, he turned the whole package over to his operations officer, Commander John R. Millett, another Naval Academy graduate and *Missouri's* third in command. "Here John," he said, "you take care of this."

Commander Millett didn't even open the envelope. He turned it over to the ship's navigating officer, Lieutenant Commander Frank G. Morris. Morris, a thin-faced, youngish looking man with intense blue eyes, had joined the Navy in 1940 as an apprentice seaman in the V-7 program and risen through the ranks. He had joined the *Missouri* only two days before the pre-Christmas shakedown cruise, and apparently his performance of duty hadn't impressed Captain Brown favorably. The captain felt the navigator relied too heavily on Loran (radio bearings) for his position fixes, and he had been several miles off on his landfall when the *Missouri* returned from her sea trials. That is why he asked the operations officer, whom

he trusted fully, to check out the acoustical range run. Unfortunately he hadn't told either Millett or Morris of his feelings in this regard.

The following day, January 14, Captain Brown called a conference with his operations and navigating officers for eleven o'clock in the morning. Morris arrived on time; Millett some five minutes late. Most of the conversation dealt with general details of *Missouri's* voyage to Cuba, the running of the acoustical range being discussed only briefly. Such casualness is difficult to understand when it is considered that the run would put the huge superdreadnaught on the "wrong" side of the heavily traveled ship channel in restricted waters beset by shoals, a maneuver somewhat like trying to run a diesel over-the-road truck through a motorcycle obstacle course.

Morris insists that he discussed the acoustical range marker buoys with the captain. Actually, there were only two . . . orange and white striped globes not much bigger than large beach balls. They floated just on the safe side of a "danger bearing" . . . an imaginary straight line between Old Point Comfort light and Thimble Shoal light. To the right of the danger bearing a ship was safe in 50 to 60 feet of water, but if she crossed the line inside the left-hand buoy she would find herself in fast-shoaling water.

Originally there had been five buoys marking the range. Three of these had been removed just two days before Captain Brown took command of the *Missouri*. According to Morris, he pointed out the twin buoy pattern, marked in red ink on the chart, but he had not erased three lightly-penciled symbols for the buoys that were no longer there, having received no authorization to do so.

Regardless of who said what, the *Missouri's* captain and operations officer left the conference convinced that five buoys marked the acoustical range, including two entrance buoys and two exit buoys. The run seemed simple enough. The battleship had only to steam between the two entrance buoys, steer toward the two exit buoys a mile or so ahead, and pass between them before turning right to regain the normal ship channel.

At seven o'clock on the morning of January 17, U.S.S. *Missouri* lay at the south side of Norfolk Naval Base Pier 7, gently blowing off steam and ready to sail for Guantanamo . . . via the Hampton Roads Acoustical Range. All water tanks were full, fuel tanks 95 percent full and ammunition fully loaded. The huge ship, loaded as she was, weighed 57,000 tons and drew 35 feet nine inches at the bow; 36 feet nine inches at the stern. Captain Brown, in the closet-sized chart room aft of the eighth level navigating bridge and wheelhouse, inspected the chart of Chesapeake Bay laid out neatly on the table by Lieutenant Commander Morris, the navigator. It was the first time he had looked at it since the meeting three days before, and the first time he had seen the navigator's proposed track through the acoustical range and the red "danger bearing" marking the line between Old Point Comfort and Thimble Shoal.

Captain R. B. McCoy, the civilian Navy Yard pilot who would undock the *Missouri,* joined Captain Brown on the upper level control center. This location, eight decks above the main deck in the battleship's towering forward mast structure, was used for conning the ship in restricted waters, since the view aft was less restricted than at lower levels. Once in more open waters, control was shifted to another more spacious bridge and wheelhouse at Level Four. Also gathered in the tiny wheelhouse, even smaller chart room and small open bridge at Level Eight were Commander George E. Peckham, the ship's executive officer, the operations officer, navigator, communications officer, assistant navigator and junior and senior officers of the deck, as well as the enlisted men of the special sea detail . . . helmsman, quartermasters, lookouts and "talkers." Peckham, although second in command, and the only officer with long service aboard the *Missouri,* had never been informed of the plans to run the acoustical range. As far as he knew, *Mighty Mo* was departing for a routine voyage to Cuba.

Eleven levels below the bridge, in the armor-encased Combat Operations Center, Lieutenant John E. Carr, the ship's COC officer, was preparing for a monotonous watch. A 1943 graduate of Annapolis and World War II submariner, Carr was aware that he was responsible for the battleship's secondary navigational, gunnery and combat intelligence center, but he didn't expect to have much to do until the *Missouri* cleared the harbor and began scheduled gunnery drill. It was standard procedure for all navigation of the ship to be handled from the bridge in clear weather, without additional information from the Combat Operations Center's radar, fathometer or plot readings. So

confident was Lieutenant Carr that his advice and counsel wouldn't be required that he had gotten out a shore bombardment chart rather than a regular navigational chart. On this, John W. Spooner, Quartermaster First Class, would maintain radar plot of the ship's progress. Lieutenant Wallace Van Pelt was also in COC, but his was the role of innocent bystander. He was slated to relieve Carr and was there as an observer to familiarize himself with the operations of the center.

Even lower in the *Missouri's* massive hull, well below the waterline, the chief engineering officer, Commander R. A. Zoeller and his assistant, Lieutenant James N. Forehan, stood by to receive the signals from the bridge which would set their huge steam turbines to work.

At 7:25, Captain Brown ordered all lines cast off. Puffing Navy Yard tugs put their shoulders to the massive bulk of the *Missouri,* drew her from the dock and turned her on her course. The weather was fine . . . a few scattered clouds, but visibility of at least ten miles, and the wind variable from two to 20 knots. McCoy, the civilian pilot, found the ship responding nicely to his orders.

At 7:49, off Elizabeth River Channel Buoy 3, Captain McCoy turned the con over to Captain Brown and descended the jacob's ladder to an accompanying tug for the return to Norfolk. Captain Brown rang the engines up to two-thirds speed and, at the recommendation of Morris, the navigator, ordered a course of 053 degrees toward the acoustical range. Bevan E. Travis, Quartermaster Second Class, had served as helmsman aboard the *Missouri* for nearly three years, and he knew how to handle her. He swung the wheel over and *Mighty Mo* settled gracefully on her new course. Senior Chief Quartermaster L. E. Reams, standing beside Travis and keeping a seasoned eye on the helm, nodded his approval.

Aft of the wheelhouse to starboard, in the chart room, twenty-three year old Ensign E. R. Harris, a Naval R.O.T.C. graduate of Villanova University, rather nervously marked off the ship's progress on the chart. Regularly assigned as signal officer, he had been appointed temporary assistant navigator only a few days before. His only experience in plotting the course of a ship under way had been on the brief shakedown cruise in December. Two quartermasters, Robert Hess and Ward Folansby, were on the bridge taking bearings, which they relayed to Ensign Harris via the bearing recor-

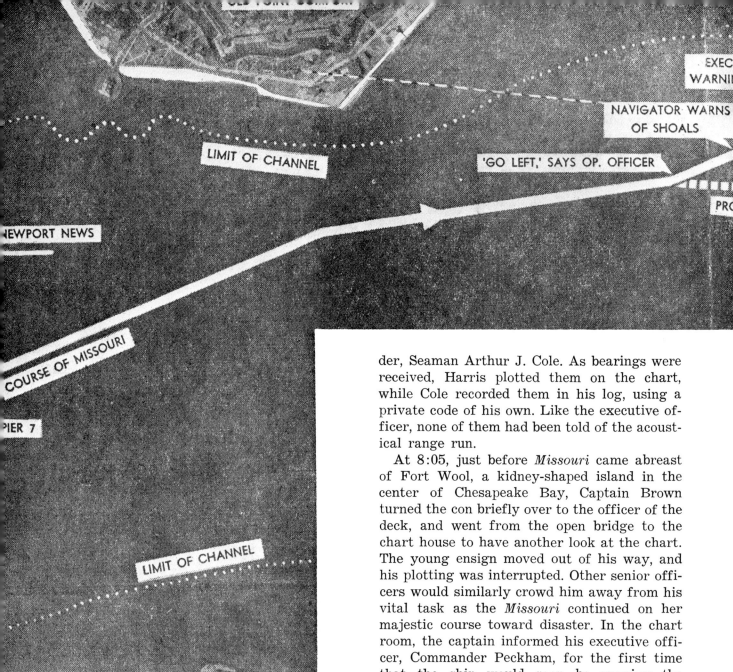

EXEC.
WARNIN(

NAVIGATOR WARNS
OF SHOALS

LIMIT OF CHANNEL

'GO LEFT,' SAYS OP. OFFICER

NEWPORT NEWS

PRO

COURSE OF MISSOURI

PIER 7

LIMIT OF CHANNEL

FORT WOOL

52 MINUTES OF MIXUP ON MIGHTY MO. This Navy aerial photo from 11,000 foot altitude was diagramed by newspaper artist to show how the **MISSOURI,** far right, got out of the channel and into the shallow waters of Thimble Shoal.

der, Seaman Arthur J. Cole. As bearings were received, Harris plotted them on the chart, while Cole recorded them in his log, using a private code of his own. Like the executive officer, none of them had been told of the acoustical range run.

At 8:05, just before *Missouri* came abreast of Fort Wool, a kidney-shaped island in the center of Chesapeake Bay, Captain Brown turned the con briefly over to the officer of the deck, and went from the open bridge to the chart house to have another look at the chart. The young ensign moved out of his way, and his plotting was interrupted. Other senior officers would similarly crowd him away from his vital task as the *Missouri* continued on her majestic course toward disaster. In the chart room, the captain informed his executive officer, Commander Peckham, for the first time that the ship would soon be running the acoustical range.

Within two minutes, Captain Brown was back on the open bridge, where he summoned the officer of the deck for the morning watch, Lieutenant Hatfield, and the relieving officer of the deck for the forenoon watch, Lieutenant Arnold, and told them to keep a sharp watch for acoustical range marker buoys. This being the first either had heard of the range or its buoys, they looked understandably puzzled. Captain Brown snapped, "Go and get yourselves informed." They beat an abashed retreat to the chart house, crowded Ensign Harris again (more than three people in *Missouri's* Level Eight Chart Room constitute a crowd), and noted the cluster of buoys penciled and red-

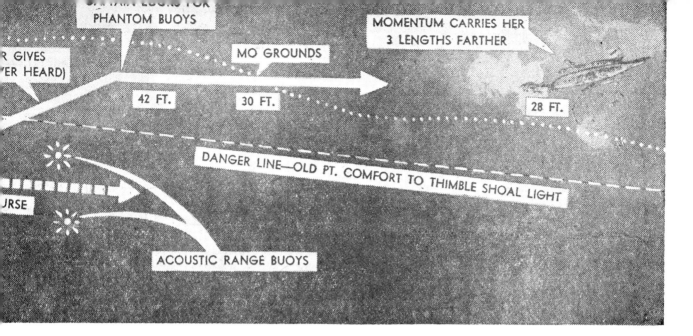

PHANTOM BUOYS

R GIVES
ER HEARD)

MO GROUNDS

MOMENTUM CARRIES HER
3 LENGTHS FARTHER

42 FT.

30 FT.

28 FT.

DANGER LINE—OLD PT. COMFORT TO THIMBLE SHOAL LIGHT

JRSE

ACOUSTIC RANGE BUOYS

inked on the chart. They returned to the bridge still somewhat confused.

At 8:10, the captain ordered a course change to 060 degrees, but a strong current swung the ship too far right, and a correction was made to 058 degrees. At about the same time he told Commander Peckham that the con would remain at Level Eight until the range run had been completed. It had been customary aboard the *Missouri* to shift control down to Level Four while in the channel between Old Point Comfort and Fort Wool. The executive officer went below to prepare for the change-over, but first he stepped into the Chart Room, took a quick look at the ship's track, rapidly approaching the danger bearing, and told Morris, "For God's sake, watch it!"

The captain asked the navigator and operations officer, as the ship rapidly closed on the range, whether it would be advisable to increase speed to 15 knots. Millett was under the impression that speed should be reduced to five knots, but Morris was sure that any steady speed was all right. The captain felt the battleship would answer her helm better at higher speed, and Millett agreed that there was plenty of water under the keel for a fast run, so Captain Brown ordered the engine room anunciators rung up to standard speed. The engine room crew responded smartly and the 180,000-horsepower turbines of *Mighty Mo* hummed at a higher pitch as they built up toward 15 knots. She continued to accelerate throughout the few minutes left to her.

As the *Missouri* began to pick up speed, Lieutenant Arnold sighted a small round buoy with orange and white stripes 1,000 yards almost dead ahead. He reported to the captain, who conferred with the operations officer. Both misidentified it as one of the nonexistent buoys and agreed that it would be safe to pass to the left of it. Lieutenant Arnold had, in the meantime, made out the letter "B" on the buoy, and so reported to the captain, but like a good deal of other information that day, the report was either not heard or was disregarded.

The "B" designation marked this as the left-hand entrance buoy of the acoustical range . . . the one nearest the shoals. From the moment Captain Brown ordered a left rudder course change to 053 degrees to pass to the left of that buoy, *Missouri* was in grave danger.

Forward superstructure. Arrow indicates Level Eight bridge.
. . . photo by Judy Kay Wilson

DECK VIEW of U.S.S. **MISSOURI** soon after her stranding on Thimble Shoal.

By this time Brown and Millett, as well as the officer of the deck, had observed two spar buoys a mile ahead. The captain and operations officer assumed they were the also nonexistent exit buoys, marking the end of the acoustical range. These were actually stakes driven into the sand, marking a shallow fishing channel through Thimble Shoal, a fact known, by their black and white markings, to Arnold, Peckham and several quartermasters, but their opinion was never asked. Captain Brown did inquire of the officers near him what they thought about the spar buoys, but the inquiry wasn't addressed to anyone in particular, and there was no reply.

Convinced that they marked the exit from the range, the *Missouri's* commander thenceforth kept her towering bow aimed dead between them, her quadruple screws thundering at an ever increasing tempo as they drove her 45,000-ton hull, carrying 12,000 tons and draw-

ing 36 feet of water, toward a fishboat channel with a depth of 14 feet.

As the battleship swung further left, Navigator Morris approached the captain looking worried. "Although I haven't seen the buoys, I recommend that the ship come right."

Captain Brown frowned. "The buoys are right ahead," he said. "We can't come right without running them down."

At 8:15, with the orange and white entrance buoy close off the starboard bow, *Missouri* crossed the danger bearing. Morris again went to the captain and said, "The bearing is getting high. I recommend coming right NOW!" To this urgent plea the captain made no reply at all, and later could not recall having heard it.

Now thoroughly alarmed, Morris took a bearing on Thimble Shoal light and rushed back to the captain, waving his arms and shouting, "COME RIGHT! THERE'S SHOAL WATER AHEAD!"

74

Captain Brown looked disapprovingly at the excited lieutenant commander and told Commander Millett, "I don't believe the navigator knows where we are. Go check his position."

Both Millett and Morris rushed to the chart house, shouldered the unfortunate Ensign Harris aside again, and consulted the chart. There they remained as the drama reached its climax.

The captain decided to make a precautionary course change while Millett and Morris checked the chart. He ordered Quartermaster Travis to bring her ten degrees right, to 063 degrees. Even had the order been allowed to stand, the change would have been too little and too late. As the *Missouri's* towering bow swung right in answer to the rudder change, Brown lined up her jackstaff between the two spar buoys ahead and asked the quartermaster for a mark of the heading being passed. "058 degrees, sir," was the answer. "Very well," the captain ordered. "Steady up on 058 degrees."

Travis swung the wheel back to the left, but for the first time in the three years he had known her, *Mighty Mo* did not respond obediently and gracefully to his hand upon her helm. Instead of coming left, the great bow continued to turn stubbornly to the right . . . to 065 degrees before it began a sluggish response to the rudder. It was is if *Mighty Mo,* being driven toward disaster, was making a last minute effort to save herself.

As Travis swung the wheel hard over to the left, he told Chief Quartermaster Reams, *"I think she's going aground".*

He was only one of a number of officers and enlisted men who were aware that their ship was in grave danger. But the captain, backed by two centuries of naval tradition and authority, was in command, and he gave no indication of doubt or fear. Actually, he was to testify later, he felt "utterly alone" at that moment . . . that his command team had failed him and that he was getting neither advice nor vital information.

When the *Missouri* had completed her brief post-overhaul run in December, Commander Peckham had approached the new captain with a number of suggestions which he felt would improve efficiency, but the commanding officer had not received them well. He told his executive officer, "George, I know your recommendations were meant well, but I am the captain and you are the executive officer and administrator." Peckham had relayed this information to the operations and navigation officers and

Showing her boot topping.

75

LADY IN TROUBLE. Blowing off steam and immodestly showing ten feet of her underwear, **MIGHTY MO** is pictured here five hours after her stranding. She struck at high tide. This photograph was taken near the afternoon low tide, with a tanker alongside pumping out fuel oil to lighten ship.

FLAGS DROOPING and radar antenna stilled, **MIGHTY MO** lies forlornly on the shoal. Radar plots from the antenna above the battle mast were inaccurate, but still showed the battleship steaming toward shallow water.

FROM 800 FEET UP, the **MISSOURI** looked like this at 4.30 on the afternoon of her stranding. The first of the fleet of tugs which would assemble around her had already come to her aid, but it would be another two weeks before they could pull her free.

added that Brown "had bawled me out". A battleship is somewhat like a small town. News travels fast, and all hands were no doubt aware that Captain Brown didn't encourage unsolicited advice.

In the meantime, Commander Peckham, down on Level Four, watched Quartermaster Harold A. Rice make his plot of the ship's course on a navigational chart. As the penciled track advanced, so did the executive officer's alarm. When the *Missouri* changed course to 053 degrees to pass the entrance buoy, he ordered his telephone talker, Seaman William D. Freeze, to transmit a message to the captain on the upper bridge . . . "The executive recommends turning right."

Stationed as talker in the upper wheelhouse was Apprentice Seaman Arden A. Field, Jr., who received the message from Freeze. He stuck his head out an open port hole and relayed it, in the face of an 18-mile-an-hour head wind, to Captain Brown, who was talking to the navigator and didn't acknowledge it. At the subsequent naval court of inquiry into the events of that day, Seaman Field frustrated and enraged the admirals of the board by mumbling so badly that they couldn't hear anything he said. As a matter of fact, two out of three of the men assigned duties as "talkers" aboard the *Missouri* were subsequently found to be very poor talkers indeed.

At 8:15, as the battleship crossed the danger bearing, Peckham transmitted another urgent message to the captain. "Ship heading into dangerous shoals. Recommend you come right immediately!"

Three minutes later he dropped naval courtesy and sent the message, *"Come right immediately! Twist ship!"*[1]

---

1. If this order had been accepted, the *Missouri's* starboard engines would have been reversed, the port engines set full ahead, and the rudder swung hard right, thus effecting a radical turn to the right. Even this emergency measure would have been useless, for the *Missouri* was already traveling "overland".

Five levels up, Seaman Field dutifully stuck his head out the port and relayed these messages to Captain Brown, who again gave no indication that he heard them. As the *Missouri* continued to bear left toward the shoals, Peckham dashed to the 21 M.C. loudspeaker microphone and shouted a recommendation to "back all engines full". No one on the upper bridge recalled hearing this, either.

Missouri's path toward the shoals was being plotted at still another location, in Combat Operations Center below decks. Radar bearings were marked on the shore bombardment chart by Quartermaster Spooner in preparation for the gunnery drill scheduled for 8:30 that morning. The radar wasn't properly calibrated, so Spooner's course was from 400 to 700 yards off the ship's true course. Even so, the COC chart, like those of Ensign Harris at Level Eight, and Commander Peckham at Level Four, clearly showed the *Missouri* headed for shoal water.

Apprentice Seaman John Beeman was manning the fathometer in Combat Operations Center. This electronic device recorded the depth of water under the ship's keel at any given moment, but it had broken down after the *Missouri* left the Naval Base. Seaman Beeman had been minding the fathometer since 1948 and nobody had once asked him for a reading, so he didn't bother to report that it wasn't working.

The Combat Operations Center personnel had been told not to bother the bridge with navigational reports unless they were asked for. So they watched the plot march across the chart toward Thimble Shoal and wondered what was going on topside. It was generally agreed that the radar must be more out of kilter than they had thought.

Far above and forward, Apprentice Seaman John Williams stood his special sea detail watch in the chains (a platform at the ship's side near the bow for taking depth soundings by the old fashioned hand lead), but he had received no orders to take soundings. In any event, the battleship was steaming so fast by this time that his lead line would have been useless.

On the bridge, Captain Brown received no reports of water depths, so he assumed that they were normal.

At 8:17, with the *Missouri* still completing her reluctant turn to the left, her bow first touched the sand, but such was her momentum that she did not falter or slacken speed. Seaman Robert Shiflet, after lookout at Level Six, saw mud kicking up astern of the ship and relayed the information to the talker on the bridge. Again, Captain Brown failed to get the message, and it was relayed to him by Arnold, the officer of the deck.

Almost simultaneously, the engine room watch reported loss of vacuum and firemain pressure. The engines were still at standard speed, but they were slowing of their own accord. Again, it seemed as if *Might Mo*, betrayed by the human errors of her ship's company, was trying to save herself.

Receiving no orders from the bridge, Chief Engineer Zoeller repeated the information two minutes later, adding that power was dropping to zero. Much too late, Captain Brown ordered "Right full rudder".

Then the engine room anunciators clanged into life with a wild flurry of orders:

Stop starboard engine!
All engines back two-thirds!
All engines back full!

But Commander Zoeller had shut the engines down. Sand and mud, instead of water, were coming in all the intakes, and would soon do lethal damage to the machinery.

Running at twelve and half knots and still

MISSOURI aground, salvage craft at work (Schematic drawing).

accelerating, *Mighty Mo* had struck the hard-packed sand of Thimble Shoal, literally lifted herself six feet out of the water and glided, like some mammoth amphibian, three ships-lengths "inland".

Like the great lady she had always been, *Missouri* grounded gracefully, knocking no one off his feet and coming to rest on an almost even keel. To a casual viewer who did not notice that six feet of her boot-topping was above water, she would have seemed serenely at anchor in deep water. Her captain and most of her crew were not even aware that she was aground until it was all over. She had struck near the crest of an exceptionally high tide.

In the organizational structure of the Atlantic Fleet, *Missouri* came under the broad command of Admiral Smith as Commander, Cruisers, Atlantic. About forty-five minutes after she went aground, word of her plight reached him during a conference on the second floor of his Norfolk headquarters. From the rear windows of that floor, he could see what his mind momentarily refused to believe. It was no mirage. There she was, jammed on Thimble Shoal between Old Point Comfort and Thimble Shoal light . . . the most prominent marker in the harbor.

The pride of the U.S. Navy lay in plain view of tens of thousands of people on both sides of Hampton Roads. Without much eye-straining, ten shore-based admirals could see her from the upper stories of their quarters on Dillingham Boulevard . . . the "Gold Dust Row of the Naval Brass." Even worse, she was in equally plain view of as many high-ranking Army officers at Fortress Monroe.

Always a realist, Admiral Smith turned sadly to his staff. "Gentlemen", he said, "U.S.S. *Missouri* has just gone half a mile inland".

DRESS REHEARSAL for **MISSOURI'S** ultimate rescue was held on the afternoon of January 31, 1950. This photograph was taken from 1,500 feet.

Chapter Seven

"How Do You Move The RCA Building?"

DOZENS OF SHIPS, naval and commercial, have gone aground in Hampton Roads, where modern naval history began with the duel between the ironclads *Monitor* and *Merrimac,* and from which the first *Missouri* set out upon her ill-fated crossing of the Atlantic. But none had presented such a colossal salvage problem as did *Mighty Mo.* Nor had any battleship done it before.

This was no ordinary mishap. The only comparable peacetime stranding of a battleship was that of the U.S.S. *Colorado* 23 years earlier in New York's East River. But the *Colorado* had been freed in a day. Admiral Smith, viewing the sad plight of *Mighty Mo,* was under no delusion that her refloating would be simple.

He knew, too, that every move made by the Navy now would be made in the glare of world-wide publicity. Lying hard aground on Thimble Shoal was America's newest battleship, and the only active one in the fleet. The Navy's salty souls loved her with a fierce devotion. Ordinary citizens had high regard for her, too, as the foremost historical monument of the century. Yet suddenly she had become the ship that launched a thousand bad jokes.

Newspaper and radio humorists referred to her as the "world's biggest stick in the mud". They said it was the first time in naval history that a battleship had hit a bar the sailors didn't like . . . that the new Navy recruiting slogan would be "Join the Navy and see Thimble Shoal" . . . that plans were afoot to cement her in permanently as "Fort Missouri" . . . that the name of President Truman's favorite song was being changed from "Missouri Waltz" to "Missouri Wake" . . . that her crew's time was now being counted as shore leave.

Red Fleet, official publication of the Soviet Navy, announced joyfully that *Missouri's* stranding "demonstrates the low level of American naval technique", as well as proving that "the level of naval culture and qualifications of ship's crew as well as that of American organization and salvaging services are far from exemplary".

Admiral Smith knew there would be a lot of tidying up to do in the aftermath of the *Missouri's* public embarrassment, including a court of inquiry and, it seemed inevitable, courts-martial of those responsible for her plight.

But the primary task was that of getting her afloat again. Many high ranking naval officers favored hiring a large commercial salvage firm to do the job, but Smith wouldn't go along with that opinion. The Navy had put *Might Mo* ashore. It was up to the Navy to get her off. He had his way, but it was made abundantly clear that he had better be right. If the Navy's salvage efforts proved to be another fiasco he would find himself extremely unpopular at the Pentagon.

Admiral Smith's decision to take on the salvage job himself was influenced to no small degree by the presence at Norfolk, as Navy Yard commandant, of Rear Admiral Homer N. Wallin. As a captain, Wallin had been in charge of salvaging the ships blasted at Pearl Harbor by the Japanese sneak attack of December 7, 1941. Nineteen of the 21 warships that had been written off as total wrecks were refloated by Wallin and his men, and refitted to fight again.

The former Pearl Harbor salvage officer was as anxious as Smith to see the Navy reestablish itself in the public's confidence, and he pledged his wholehearted assistance in getting the *Missouri* afloat again.

The following is a report on that remarkable

THREE-RING CIRCUS had nothing on the manifold operations which took place aboard the **MISSOURI** as all possible weight was removed. While anchor chains are prepared for removal in the foreground, a floating crane prepares to remove ammunition, left, and a water lighter, right, pumps fresh water from the ship's tanks.

salvage job by the man who was in charge of it, Admiral Allan E. Smith:

"How would you go about moving the R.C.A. Building a distance of one-half mile?

"The main R.C.A. building of Rockefeller Center is 850 feet high. The USS MISSOURI is 888 feet long. The MISSOURI's 57,000 tons approaches the weight of the Rockefeller Center building. The MISSOURI's underwater body takes up about the same amount of space as the Rockefeller Center Building. Though the problem of moving the grounded MISSOURI one-half mile is not the same as moving the Rockefeller Center Building the same distance, the comparisons given indicate the magnitude of the problem.

"When I boarded the MISSOURI late Tuesday afternoon, the day she grounded, I had to climb ten feet up the jacob's ladder from the

small boat, and then I was only on the lower platform of the regular ship's gangway. She was out of the water a distance from the ground floor of a house to the middle of the second floor—10 feet, and the extra distance showing weighed about the equivalent of a new heavy cruiser—17,000 tons. It was apparent at once to me that there could be no "quickie" solution.

"Falling back on my wartime experience of estimating the situation, arriving at a decision, and then implementing that decision, the following major factors controlled:—

"(1) Except for an abnormal northeast

81

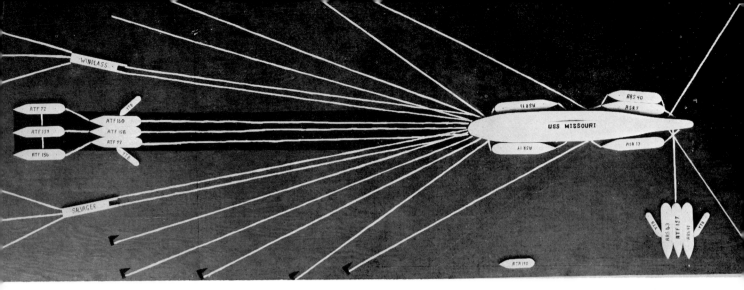

Labels on diagram: WINDLASS, ATF 72, ATF 151, ATF 156, ATF 160, ATF 158, ATF 77, SALVAGER, USS MISSOURI, ARS 40, ARS 7, ARS 16, ARS 14, ARS 13, ARS 43, ATF 157, ARS 46, ATR 110

wind, the high tides would not be up again until the 2nd of February.

"(2) I had to stay within the means available, which were—dredging, diving, tunneling, use of beach gear and pontoons, and pulling or pushing by tugs.

"So the basic plan came down to the following:

(1) Take sufficient readily removable weights out of her so that the high tide which would be available on 2 February would approach the amount of water necessary to float her.

(2) Lift her up by various means so that she does not need so much water to float her.

(3) Remove some of the hard-packed, concrete-like sand from under her so that she can squash down to let the high tide of 2 February reach her better.

(4) To get her free, use sheer force to make up the difference between the needed water height and the weights which could not be removed.

(5) Once afloat, to have a dredged channel to deep water.

"First, we unloaded 8,000 tons of fuel in order to ease the pressure on the sand and gravel underneath, much of which had been compressed to a composition approaching concrete. Then a half dozen divers went down in the strong tides with hydraulic hoses having water pressure of 200 to 300 pounds per square inch and began breaking down the hard-packed sand. This was a slow, difficult, and time-consuming job in view of the volume of sand and gravel beneath the ship and in consideration of the date—2 February.

SALVAGE PLAN: Streaming from the **MISSOURI'S** deck were nine two-inch steel hawsers secured to heavy anchors well placed and running to winches secured to the deck. This was the beach gear. Two special steel hawsers, one on each quarter, were made fast to submarine salvage ships, both with two special Danforth anchors out. These salvage ships could pull in both directions. Astern were six tugs in a tandem of three abreast. Both "nests" had a smaller tug to keep them on their pulling axis. On the bow were three tugs to give a "whipsaw" effect. On each side were several tugs fitted in between all the steel cables and the pontoons.

YW 119, a yard water lighter, pumps fresh water from the **MISSOURI** during lighten ship operations. Two YT-type harbor tugs are alongside.

U.S.NAVY YW 119

PASS THE AMMUNITION. Floating crane removing anchors, chain and ammunition from the **MISSOURI.**

"We dredged a trench 35 to 40 feet down all around the ship. The Army Dredge COMBER with its alert crew and administration dug this excellent trench so that the hard-packed sand could be pushed into it when the base upon which the MISSOURI rested was cracked or broken. There was no dredge available in the area which was capable of getting under the hull, but we contracted for a commercial dredge which could get close alongside and a little bit under the stern.

"Divers dug two holes about ten feet into the ground and about fifty feet from the sides of the ship, and a charge of 75 pounds of T.N.T. was exploded in each of these. This jolted the ship and the sand base, and the ship settled one inch almost immediately. One inch of freeboard is worth 150 tons (the weight of about 80 of your brand of automobile).

"We followed this up by continued tunneling and taking out all readily removable fluids and weights to the extent of 4,600 tons. Nothing removable remained except the crew, whose total weight amounted to less than one inch. Because both the crew and our officers wished to stand by the ship, I gave the orders that they were not to disembark unless it was one of our last hopes.

"Now the tides—There are two high tides each day, one of these being higher than the other, but starting with the day the ship went aground the highest tide failed to reach that of the previous day by an inch or two, and this continued for about a week. Then the highest tide each day began to go up again and on 2 February reached within one inch of that when

PONDEROUS PROJECTILES are removed from a 16-inch magazine . . .

positioned under a handling hatch . . .

hoisted above decks . . .

manhandled to the floating crane . . .
and stowed neatly on a barge alongside.

Propelling charges for 16-inch guns hoisted above decks for transfer to barge.

the MISSOURI went aground. It was plain, therefore, that if we could get our basic plans completed and our organization formed, and the salvage gear and personnel concentrated in time to implement our basic plan by 2 February, we had a fair chance of success. So I committed myself and the Navy to refloat the MISSOURI by 2 February, and as standards exist in our Navy I new that failure meant there would be new faces not later than 4 February —as the lawyers put it, 'Time was of the essence'.

"While we were planning, organizing, concentrating the men, ships, and gear, the weather showed that a northeaster would blow up about the morning of 20 January, which might give a tide higher than the book indicated. Because this would not interfere with our longer range plan, I arranged for a pull, using as many tugs as we could obtain in the area, with the knowledge that our computations showed that unless it was an extraordinarily high tide, the ship would not come off. This turned out to be a fact, but we had gained some experience in coordination for the greater test later.

"With me on board I had my Chief of Staff, Captain Roland N. Smoot; my Operations Officer; and one or two others of the Staff. One of my first dispatches was to ask the Army District Engineer, Colonel G. W. Derby, for the Dredge, COMBER, which was doing routine maintenance work in the Baltimore Channel. The next day the COMBER was on the job dredging around the MISSOURI.

"On the second day I sent a dispatch to Rear Admiral Homer N. Wallin, whose regular as-

signment is that of Commander of the Norfolk Naval Shipyard. We were shipmates on a staff at Pearl Harbor in 1941, after which we were separated and he became the Salvage Officer for the Pearl Harbor ships. As his authority lead straight to the Shipyard, the desirability of having him as a Deputy was apparent, and I requested the Commandant, FIFTH Naval District to issue Temporary Additional Duty orders to Rear Admiral Wallin as such. Also, I secured two Lieutenant Commanders, one experienced in pontoons and the other in beach gear.

"I started staff conferences at 11:00 A.M. and 5:00 P.M. daily, and these usually lasted 1-1½ hours. These conferences insured that our basic plan was followed and that the flexibility needed to meet the daily change in situation was inherent. In an operation of this type with a time schedule—once a proper estimate of the situation is made and a decision reached, then the basic plan must be adhered to; else the many, many parts will start conflicting with each other, delays will occur, the basic plan will fall apart. Only an unexpected major factor which strikes directly at the basic plan should cause one to change his major decision.

"The Chief of Staff drew up a time-space diagram, similar to that used in large industrial plants, so that we knew exactly when a water barge, fuel barge, tanker, a tug for divers, or any other type of ship would be alongside, and in this manner could have the next ship already to slide in when another pulled away. We brought in the Chief Pilot of the Norfolk Naval Base to our conferences, so that we could have

Deck scene on the **MISSOURI** during off-loading of ammunition.

complete mutual understanding and purpose behind each move. I was forced to carry along one member who had an important job—who did not seem to have the knack of readily accomplishing his tasks; and the same problem frequently appears in any great war operations where a time factor is involved—Do you keep the officer who has all the information in his head and strengthen him, or do you get a new one who might be better but who lacks the information and cannot possibly gain the value of the history of the case which the other has? In this case, I kept him and gave him more assistance.

"The establishment of a base line of what the draft of the ship actually was when she went aground, and from which to predict the tide and also any movement of the ship required considerable computation and ingenuity —this was undertaken by Rear Admiral Wallin.

"We knew that if the tide on 2 February failed to come up to that predicted, we had to make up the difference by our lifting and especially our pulling effort. Also, there was the additional fact that after 4 February the high tide dropped away completely and would not again approach that of the date of grounding for another month—sometime in March.

"As time went on, all members of my staff understood that they must speak up if they had a worthy comment or needed a question answered, and that the discussions were helpful to the decision. Our coordination improved, as did our efficiency; and more important, we

SIXTEEN-INCH projectiles off-loaded onto Navy barge.

obtained that mutual understanding—a necessity in any field of endeavor.

"There was continual interference between the dredges and the divers, since the divers could not work within 200 feet of the dredges as they might be sucked in. There was interference between the positioning of the pontoons and the dredges and getting cables under the hull in order to secure the pontoons. There was interference in the process of discharging ammunition, the loading and offloading of fuel, the taking out of the MISSOURI'S tremendous anchors and chains, bringing them back and taking them out again. All these caused interference with some other necessary effort. All of these had to be smoothed out into a continuous flow with the greatest results as the aim.

"As the days and nights went by I began a struggle to reduce the time of completion and to so funnel matters that we might be ready for the tide on 31 January, two days before the high tide on 2 February. On the night of 30 January, we turned to and produced our Operation Order with several annexes and accomplished distribution to the many tugs and other units involved, before morning. This was necessary so that everyone would have an understanding of what we were attempting and to reduce the number of orders that would have to be given.

"We had Plans "A," "B" and "C" to accomplish certain phases, such as twisting, straight pulling, surging and the like. In this way, all I had to do was say, "Execute Plan 'A'." We were not ready with our pontoons or our tunneling

FLOATING POWDER KEG. Sailors rig protective tarpaulins over bargeload of 16-inch powder charges off-loaded from MISSOURI. The skipper of the Navy harbor tug at the right is in the wheel house, ready to get under way as soon as the cargo is secured.

AN ALL-HANDS AFFAIR was the off-loading of the 2,205 tons of ammunition aboard the **MISSOURI.** These are five-inch projectiles, which weigh 70 pounds each, lightweights compared to the ton and a half of each 16-inch shell and propelling charge, but a fair load for a sailor, especially after he's moved several hundred of them.

on the morning of the 31st, but the evening before a northeaster started and as we needed the practice, we had a "Coordination Rehearsal" on the morning of 31 January.

"Going over the computations with Admiral Wallin, they looked very good, indeed, and when we failed that morning the only conclusion was that there was an unknown factor and we had not located it. Admiral Wallin thought that it was due to the fact that the ship was resting on a rock which had indented the bottom after cutting the holes in the three compartments. This may have been the case. At any rate, we shifted for the try on 1 February and pumped out the water ballast forward, which amounted to about 900 tons. This shift of weights, however, required that we gain another 29 inches aft, or an increased pull.

"There is a story that some years ago, during a storm, a car ferry lost some of her freight cars overboard in the approximate vicinity where the *Missouri* was aground. It may be that one of these freight cars is solidly imbedded in the sand and cut through the steel bottom in the three compartments. These three compartments held about 400 tons of water and we had to get it out, of course. This was done by fitting plates on the upper ends, shoring the surrounding area with heavy timbers, and then applying air pressure to force the water out through holes. This matter caused no concern either to Admiral Wallin or myself, although, because the double bottoms concerned were

fuel oil bottoms, it was a very dirty and fatiguing job for the men who did so well in accomplishing the clearing of the compartments. There are over 450 double bottoms in the U.S.S. *Missouri,* and only three of these were damaged.

"On the morning of 31 January, when we began the pull, the northeaster died down, the sea became calm, and there was a fog to contend with. We could not see the towing tugs only 1,500 feet away. One of the small tugs on the axis got across the line of one of our heaviest pulling special beach gear ships and so we lost a good part of their effort. At the same time, one of the tugs carried away our 2″ wire hawser, and reduced the effort that much more. In addition, not knowing that the nearest tugs were pulling away from the axis and the leading three tugs were pulling to 30 degrees in the opposite direction, they were far from getting a coordinated effort. Yes, the *Missouri* looked very hard aground, indeed, in the cold foggy dawn of 31 January.

"On the morning of 1 February all this had been smoothed out, and we had replaced the smaller tugs on the bow with three powerful ones. At 0530, I issued the following order— 'All Stations, ZERO HOUR is 0730'—'It is now MINUS TWO HOURS'—'Execute Plan A.' Plan 'A' gradually brought the beach gear and special beach gear ships up to full strain and also began the first pull of the three twisting tugs hauling on the starboard bow. After three minutes of this twisting movement and the tugs at full power, the *Missouri* compass showed a

Crew preparing starboard anchor chain for removal from the ship.

COMPACT POWERHOUSE. Designed to provide salvage and rescue services to wartime convoys at sea, ATR's like the **OPORTUNE** proved invaluable in **MISSOURI** salvage operations. Here she's shown preparing to drop beach gear anchor; chain and wire rope strung overside.

change of one-half degree—then one degree—then gradually more. The *Missouri* showed signs of life—her pulse quickened when I executed Plan 'B,' and she almost became unmanageable in her eagerness to display her vitality.[1]

After deck view of ATR **HOIST** from the **MISSOURI'S** deck.

---

1. A safety plan had been issued to prevent injury to the salvage crew by the heavy gear. If the *Missouri* was freed, the two-inch steel hawsers had to be cut with blow torches and, with the strain on the cables, a snapping effect would cut a man in two in a second. The decision as to when the safety plan should be put in effect was a delicate one.

Immediately after the *Missouri* began to move, the safety plan was made effective . . . and almost at once there was a terrible crunching noise on the port side. In the darkness I could see the salvage ship being crushed against the *Missouri*. Would the salvage ship be sunk and men killed?

Within two minutes the noise stopped and I received a telephone report that it was only light metal that had been damaged. The crew and ship were all clear and all right. With the first light of dawn came the final report: not a man had been injured, either in the *Missouri* or any of the salvage fleet. A feeling of thanks welled up inside me.

CIVILIAN HELP. Only non-military vessel involved in **MISSOURI** salvage was the commercial dredge **WASHINGTON,** which was able to remove sand from close under the stranded battleship.

Hoppers of the Army Engineers dredge **COMBER** filled with tons of sand and seawater as she plowed underwater trenches to help free the **MISSOURI.**

"Due to the tide and wind, the lady wanted to cut across a shoal spot and get into her own deep water, and we had to continually coax and coax her to restrain her and show her the fine deep channel that we had dredged for her. This was finally accomplished by about 7:10 A.M., and she was clear. She took on a trim of 5, then 7 feet, due to the weights we had taken out. This meant that she was seven feet deeper in the water at her stern than at the bow. I immediately gave the order to flood the tanks in the bow to counterbalance this trim, both to help get her to the deep water and because it would be needed in docking her.

"Each one of us who worked with the *Missouri* felt the exultation of her new freedom, and I gave the order to break her Battle Flags and the five flags flying from her signal halyards, which said, 'Reporting for Duty'.

"With Admiral Wallin's authority in connection with the Shipyard, he had prepared everything in advance for the *Missouri's* reception, and in one of the best jobs ever done in peace

UNDERWATER EXPLOSIVE charge being rigged to be set off close aboard the **MISSOURI.**

THOUSANDS OF DEAD FISH dot the waters of Chesapeake Bay following the underwater explosions set off to help free the **MIS- SOURI.**

BARGE LOAD OF PONTOONS comes alongside the stranded **MISSOURI** . . .

or wartime, had the *Missouri* fixed up and out of the dock in five days.

"The *Missouri* has had her dock test of engines, gone to sea and had a full power run, and shows no evidence of anything wrong. In fact, she had some vibration before she grounded and it is now reported that there is less of it.

"The officers and crew have again turned to —worked day and night to reload her ammunition, stores, fuel, water—and with one day to catch their breath, sailed as previously scheduled for Guantanamo. On 1 March she joined the PORTREX Operation, a combined training exercise of the Army, Navy and Air Force, under a unified command.

"In a careful search over a period of a week, taking sonar soundings and employing divers, we were unable to locate the object which cut the hole in the *Missouri's* hull.

"The grounding and refloating of the U.S.S. *Missouri* spotlights the personnel problems with which the Navy has been struggling in the past few years.

"The Navy has had two demobilizations since World War II—the first because our nation said everyone must get home at once—regardless. The second was caused by the first emergency, when it was considered necessary to enlist men for two years only. The two years expired and half the enlisted personnel were discharged.

"In World War II, 84% of our officers were reserves; only 14% were regulars. In 1950, the 14% regulars had been joined by sufficient reserves to make 65% of the officer personnel. In order to broaden the experience and resume the education of officers, the assignments to the Fleet were short—probably too short. The effort to regain our former high standard of efficiency, coupled with the many tasks assigned the Navy, resulted perhaps in too much activity in too little time. The pace needs some slowing. And, of course, the deficiencies in personnel will be carefully studied, followed by short range and long range plans to make corrections and improve ourselves.

"When World War II ended, our Navy had achieved most of its goals. Immediately, a comprehensive and well planned Naval Reserve program was successfully instituted. The preservation of the 'Moth Ball' Fleet was a high achievement in the field of technical planning and management. The Navy disposed of its surplus material in orderly fashion and retained the items that would be needed for the future. The Navy established an integrated supply system. A modernization program for our Fleet was instituted. There was developed a shipbuilding and plane design program specializing

and one is maneuvered under the stern to give added "lift" during the salvage effort.

in prototypes which would embody the accomplishments from the fields of research and development. An Operational Development Force to evaluate new weapons and techniques and to put them into workable shape for general fleet use was activated. Along with these noteworthy results, the Navy was ready and standing by in the Mediterranean and in the Far East.

"And of course, the Navy has been unified and is going ahead to solve the problems of the future and work with the Army and Air Force as the law requires.

"Like the *Missouri*, I just strayed a little out of the channel; so I now close with the other side of the picture of the *Missouri's* refloating.

"That an operation of such magnitude could be undertaken by a command and staff with little experience in salvage work; that the situation could be estimated so quickly—needs determined, and personnel and equipment procured with such dispatch; that plans and tasks could be conceived, formulated, and carried through; that the impact and influence of public relations was realized; that a target date for the refloating was set and then anticipated; that all this was done successfully and without

while beach gear winches aboard the **MISSOURI,** their lines made fast to huge anchors astern of the grounded battleship, add their power to the pull-off effort.

Temporary planking protected the **MISSOURI'S** teak decks from heavy beach gear.

a single casualty proves that the Navy's versatility is very broad, indeed, and that our basic concepts of organization, training and mutual understanding are sound and effective."[1]

So, after fifteen days aground, helplessly stranded for the whole world to see, to gape at, to speculate on and to joke about, *Mighty Mo* was freed in a display of Navy teamwork which did much to restore the prestige of that service. The huge salvage job, accomplished at the modest cost of $225,000, was the exact antithesis of the lack of planning and communication that had put her aground. Only the cost of the commercial dredge was outside government expenditures and appropriations.

Thousands of ordinary Americans breathed sighs of relief when the *Missouri* floated free. The concern of the nation was indicated by the scores of letters addressed to Admiral Smith and Admiral Wallin during the two-week salvage effort. A lady in Texas recounted a detailed and highly technical dream she had, involving the use of pumps to inject high-pressure water under the hull; a gentleman from

1. The opinions expressed herein are those of an individual—Rear Admiral Allan E. Smith, U. S. Navy—and do not necessarily represent the official views of the U. S. Navy.

HARD HAT DIVER "suits up" alongside the **MISSOURI** . . .

mounts the diving platform . . .

At one point in the diving operations Admiral Smith recalls, "I received a report that one of the divers was trapped under the stern of the **MO.** What could be done to help him? Rescue operations were begun . . . but at the end of 20 minutes came a report . . . the diver had cleared his lines; he was surfacing and was uninjured."

DIVER'S LIFELINE and air supply are carefully checked by tenders as he works under water in the narrow space between the diving vessel, right, and the **MISSOURI,** left.

and goes over the side.

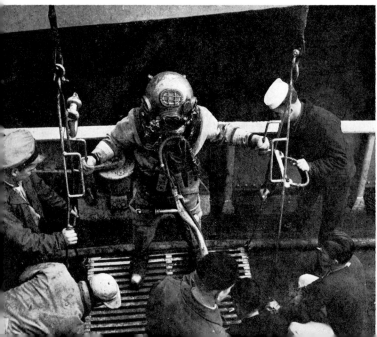

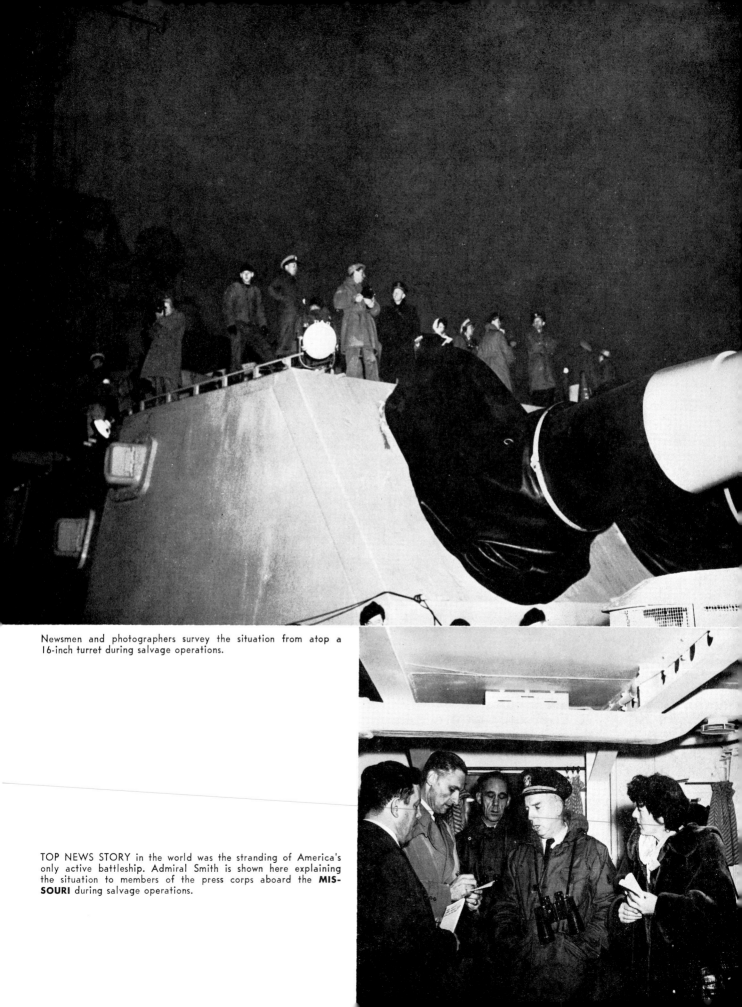

Newsmen and photographers survey the situation from atop a 16-inch turret during salvage operations.

TOP NEWS STORY in the world was the stranding of America's only active battleship. Admiral Smith is shown here explaining the situation to members of the press corps aboard the **MISSOURI** during salvage operations.

ALWAYS DARKEST JUST BEFORE THE DAWN as tugs take station for final pull-off effort at Thimble Shoal.

St. Louis suggested marshaling all the fire boats available in the area and squirting the *Mighty Mo* out of her predicament; a New Yorker urged that numerous small holes be bored in the ship's bottom and compressed air shot through them; five-year-old Loren Devine of Indianapolis dispatched a letter to Admiral Smith . . . "Dear Admiral, why can't you make the old Mo sail? Can't you fix that wreck in the bottom? Look the ship over and see if there are any holes and cracks and then write me a letter if you can make er sail. I'm worried about it."

Both Admirals Smith and Wallin answered Loren's letter, and sent him a complete set of diagrams showing how the salvage job was done. They answered all the other letters, too, from crackpots and college professors alike, including a succinct telegram from a resident of Everett, Washington, which simply directed, "Fire your guns!", and a proposal from Lans-

downe, Pennsylvania, that surplus blimps be utilized to lift *Mighty Mo* off the shoal. A number of messages offered no technical advice, but gave assurances that their senders would be praying for the U.S. Navy and the battleship *Missouri* when the final salvage effort began.

The Philadelphia *Inquirer* pretty well summed up the feelings of these and countless other citizens when *Mighty Mo* broke free and set the code flags streaming . . . "Reporting for duty":

"Freeing of the battleship *Missouri* from the mudflats off Virginia cannot fail to send thrills to the hearts of all Americans whose pride in their Navy has grown steadily throughout the glorious history of the Nation's sea forces.

"It was an unfortunate accident that sent the '*Might Mo*' aground. But it was the Navy, coming to the rescue of her own, that floated

96

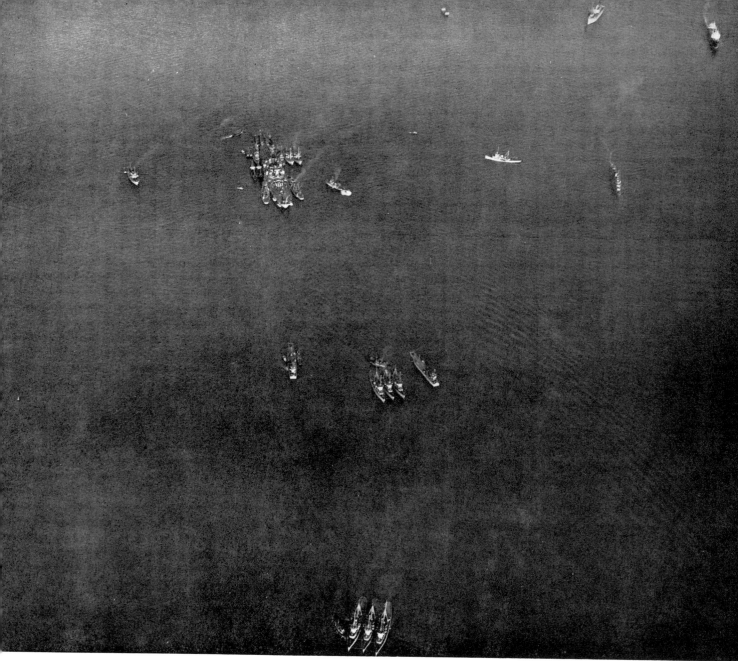

THOUSANDS OF HORSEPOWER join forces to free **MIGHTY MO** from her sandy trap in Chesapeake Bay.

the 'Mo' just as the Navy dared enemy shells and bombs to aid vessels stuck on invasion beaches in the recent war. For a moment, the unsung heroes of naval salvage operations came into the spotlight, adding a notable peacetime chapter to the illustrious record compiled in clearing the channel at Bizerte, the harbor at Cherbourg and the debris-strewn Pacific island ports.

"Here is an answer to the glib critics who are all too ready to minimize the Navy's accomplishments to bolster the cause of other components of our armed forces. Here is an answer to those too prone to write off the Navy as a useless anachronism, having no place in a world of the A-bomb, the H-bomb and air power.

"For the Navy men know their business—the infinitely complicated business of maintaining the sea forces needed for defense of the Nation. Rescuing a stricken ship is part of that business, and planning for future developments in the tactics and strategy of warfare is another.

"Great changes have come about in strategy and the employment of naval vessels since the first Navy set out to fight for the cause of American independence under John Paul Jones.

HIGH TIDE on the morning of February 1, and the little ships of the salvage fleet take their stations for the all-out effort . . . As the morning brightens, hawsers grow tight as giant fiddle-strings between the **MISSOURI** and flotilla of powerful ATR's (sea-going rescue and salvage tugs) . . .

Then, and in the years that followed, it was iron men in wooden ships, making perilous voyages to defend an infant Nation.

"But there was no change in the Navy's fundamental purpose in all the long years during which steam replaced sails, iron and steel replaced wood. Whether it was Stephen Decatur waging his battles against the Barbary pirates, the steel-clad *Monitor* locked in combat with the *Merrimac,* or a now-forgotten destroyer convoying troops to fight on Flanders fields, the aim was defense of America.

"That the Navy was ever ready to take offensive action to defeat the Nation's enemies was shown from the beginning. And there is no question that this offensive power reached a pinnacle never before attained by any nation in the last war, when the carrier forces of Mitscher and Halsey and the mighty invasion armada off Normandy became instruments of the Nation's might.

"All these should not be forgotten in the current debates over unification and the roles to be played in any future conflict by the ground forces of the Army, the planes of the Air Force and the vessels of the Navy.

"Yet there is a tendency to forget the Navy's

proud past, and its great task in carrying the fight to the enemy wherever he might be. There is a tendency to run down the Navy with intemperate attacks. There is even a tendency, now developing, to neglect the job of keeping in semi-readiness the vessels which gave us mastery of the seas in the recent war.

"Most important is the belief among Navy men that the Nation's defenses will be weakened if the role of sea power is minimized to a degree unwarranted by any sure knowledge of future combat. That belief is strengthened by the ill-advised crude crackdowns on the Navy and her top officers in recent months. It's no wonder that morale in the Navy is low.

"The Nation needs a balanced military force

for its safety—land-fighters, air-fighters and sea-fighters. It would be risking our security to build up one, at the expense of another.

"Admiral W. H. P. Blandy, retiring commander of the Atlantic Fleet, summed up the sentiments of most Americans when he addressed a 'well done' to the men who freed the 'Mighty Mo.'

"To this distinguished officer and to all others striving to keep the Navy in readiness to defend us, the Nation owes a 'well done' and more. We owe the Navy, inheritor of a proud tradition, the strongest assurance that it will be preserved and strengthened to do its job in the Nation's service."

HEADED FOR DEEP WATER, **MIGHTY MO** stirs at last from her
trap of compacted sand as salvage vessels apply full power . . .
and finally she moves freely, leaving a frothy wake behind her.
(Note flotation pontoon trailing astern).

Reporting for Duty.

WITH DEEP WATER UNDER HER KEEL, **MIGHTY MO** moves across Hamton Roads toward the Norfolk Navy Yard for drydocking and repairs.

MANNING THE RAIL, crew of ex-battleship **MISSISSIPPI** pay their respects to **MIGHTY MO** as she passes, en route to drydock.

VIEW FROM LEVEL FOUR BRIDGE as **MISSOURI** is moved toward drydock at Norfolk Navy Yard.

BOW LINES OUT, **MISSOURI** eases her bulk into the drydock for damage inspection.

QUADRUPLE PROPELLERS of the **MISSOURI** dwarf members of the naval inspection party in this stern view of the battleship in drydock.

UNDER 45,000 TONS OF BATTLESHIP, the naval photographer stood on the floor of the emptied drydock to focus his camera upward on the jagged hole in the **MISSOURI'S** bottom . . . the most serious damage done by her stranding.

MOUNTAIN OF MUD on drydock floor was sucked in through main injection pipe when **MISSOURI** grounded. Here it's shown being flushed out.

MINOR DAMAGE to starboard inboard propeller is shown in this close-up photo.

MIGHTY MO IN DRYDOCK shows bulbous underwater bow which helped her achieve 40-mile-an-hour speed. Note tiny human figures under the curve of her bilge on the drydock floor (right).

MISSOURI'S navigating officer is called as witness at inquiry into the stranding.

MISSOURI'S CAPTAIN, at the left, during interlude in board of inquiry proceedings to establish cause of ship's stranding, is questioned by press correspondents.

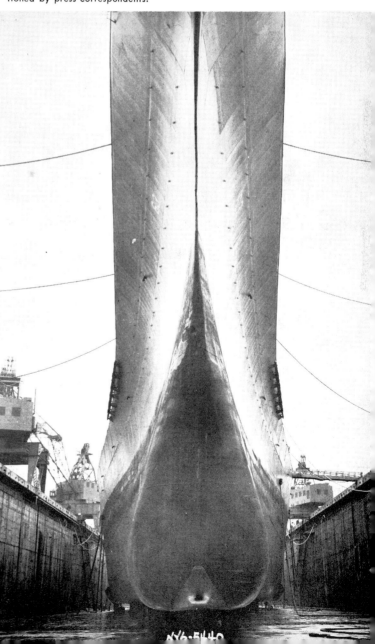

SALVAGE EXPERT, Admiral Wallin, inspects damage to **MISSOURI** in Norfolk drydock.

Chapter Eight

"The Enemy Positions Are Pulverized"

Mighty Mo suffered little physical damage from her stranding; after a few days in drydock at Norfolk, she proceeded to Exercises Portrex and Caribex Fifty, with Captain H. P. Smith temporarily back in command, but her reputuation had suffered grievously. The target of jibes and congressional criticism, there was much speculation that the Navy's last active battleship would be taken out of commission entirely.

Instead, Defense Secretary Johnson made a compromise decision. Henceforth the *Missouri* would become a school ship to train midshipmen and naval reservists. Her crew was reduced from 1,800 to 1,500, and it was estimated that her annual operating costs would be cut in half.

The naval inquiry into her grounding resulted in court martial of her captain, operations, navigating and combat intelligence center officers. All were found guilty and set back so far on the promotion lists that their naval careers were, to all extents and purposes, ended.

In March 1950, operation Caribex Fifty ended. The flag of the commander, Second Fleet, was lowered from her yardarm, and *Mighty Mo* entered her semi-retirement as a training ship under Captain I. T. Duke. In April she embarked reserves at Norfolk this time visiting New York and bringing to a total 376 reserve officers and 3,031 reserve enlisted personnel trained aboard her during the next two years.

June 25, 1950, found *Missouri* enroute to the Panama Canal Zone for the summer's first midshipman cruise. On that day another sneak attack, this time by the North Korean communist armies upon the southern Republic of Korea, changed her destiny from school ship to fighting man-of-war again.

She completed the Panama cruise and made another one to Halifax and Boston, but on August 13 she was alerted for reassignment to the combat zone. After five days of intensive rearming and replenishment at Norfolk, she steamed out of Hampton Roads and again set course for the Panama Canal. Her complement had been increased to 2,184 officers and men, including 67 marines. During her first night at sea the heavily laden battleship encountered a tropical storm which, despite evasive maneuvers and reduced speed, caused some damage topside. But *Mighty Mo* bulled her way through, and on August 23 traversed the Panama Canal. After refueling at Balboa, she headed for Pearl Harbor by the great circle route, deviating southward for two days to avoid another tropical storm. On the last day of August she docked at Pearl Harbor, where five 40-millimeter and 14 20-millimeter guns were installed to beef up her antiaircraft defenses. Within five days she had been stripped for action, conducted gunnery exercises and set sail for Sasebo, Japan.

The North Koreans had, in the meantime, followed up their initial artillery bombardments across the 38th Parallel with infantry and armored attacks against the South Koreans and the small force of American troops supporting them. The United Nations declared the attack a breach of world peace and authorized a unified force to defend the Republic of Korea, but the overwhelming attack from the north had forced defending American and South Korean troops to retreat to Pusan, where they held their ground as plans were launched for an amphibious landing of United Nations forces at Inchon.

Two days before the Inchon landing, sched-

CRASHING CRESCENDO of hurricane seas challenged **MIGHTY MO** on Korean War service as in World War II.

uled for September 15, U.S.S. *Missouri* was wallowing at five knots through the southwestern sector of typhoon "Kezia," battling 40-knot winds and tremendous swells. Captain Duke reported "radical 'tacking' into and away from the weather necessary in order to gain distance toward rendezvous and still protect helicopters aboard." *Missouri's* destination had been changed from Sasebo to a meeting at sea with the destroyers *Maddox* and *Samuel N. Moore.*

The *Missouri's* war diary for September 14, 1950, records, "Weather abated between 00001 and 04005. By dispatch at 06561 *Missouri* reported to ComNavFE (Commander of U. S. Naval forces in the Far East) for duty and to CTF 95 (Commander, Task Force 95) for operational control . . . Made rendezvous with *Maddox* and *Samuel N. Moore* at 07351. Rear Admiral Allan E. Smith, USN (CTF 95), transferred from *Maddox* and broke his flag in *Missouri* at 0747."

Task Force 95 was the designation given the United Nations Blockading and Escort Force, a well integrated unit made up of ships and men from eleven nations united in the common cause of world peace. *Mighty Mo* was now its flagship. Admiral Smith radioed a message to Tokyo and MacArthur that, unless directed otherwise, he would bombard Samchok, just below the 38th Parallel on the east coast of Korea, as a diversion from the Inchon landings.

Steaming at increased speed up the coast of Korea, escorted by the two destroyers, *Missouri* rendezvoused with the cruiser *Helena* and destroyer *Brush* just after midnight on the 15th. *Samuel N. Moore,* which had suffered damage to her forward gun mount in the heavy seas of the past two days, was sent back to Sasebo for repairs; the battleship, cruiser and

SMOKE RINGS are blown by the five-inch battery of cruiser **MANCHESTER** as she lambasts Korean shore targets in company with the **MISSOURI.**

two remaining destroyers ran in for the early morning shelling of Samchok. *Missouri* expended 52 rounds of 16-inch ammunition, each containing a ton of high explosives. Gunfire was spotted by helicopters from the flagship. Railroads and bridges were destroyed and damaged. The force then steamed south of Pohang-dong to blast other military targets in a later afternoon bombardment. As a result, the communist high command had to consider the possibility of another amphibious landing on the opposite coast from Inchon. After patrolling off the coast all night, *Missouri* made a solo bombardment run against the Pohang area, wreaking havoc to docks, warehouses and supply dumps. The communists at Pohang-dong received 90 of *Mighty Mo's* 16-inch projectiles, before she was ordered to move north to the rescue of a battalion of ROK (Republic of Korea) soldiers pinned down after their landing ship had broached on the beach and was taken under fire from the surrounding hills.

The Korean-manned LST had jammed its winch, snapped its stern anchor line and been slammed sideways on the beach by the heavy surf. Battleship, cruiser and both destroyers plastered the enemy gun emplacements inshore with five-inch gunfire throughout the night. At daybreak on September 17 the three smaller ships were left to complete the rescue, while

OVER THE WAVES, Admiral Smith transfers via "highline" from aircraft carrier **PRINCETON** to a destroyer during Task Force 95 operations off Korea.

SAD FATE of this Thailand corvette, stranded during a snow storm and taken under fire by communist shore batteries, was shared by a ROK landing ship, which broached to on the beach. All but one man of the corvette's crew were rescued by helicopter. Casualties were higher on the Korean LST, but most of its company were also rescued by the men of the **MISSOURI** and other United Nations ships.

Missouri steamed at flank speed toward the coastal city of Pohang. The United States military advisory group with the Third ROK Division on the south side of the Pohang River was under heavy attack from two and a half communist divisions and had asked for help. American observers with the ROKs ashore spotted the battleship's gunfire, directing it across the river a scant 300 yards from the friendly forces. The gunners in the 16-inch turrets poured in 298 rounds of precision fire in thirty minutes and the observers ashore radioed, "The enemy positions are pulverized and ROK

troops advancing standing up over a bridge across the river."[1]

Then *Mighty Mo* turned and raced back to the stranded ROK landing ship. Most of the ROK force . . . 725 men . . . were rescued, although 81 were killed. Soon after 10 o'clock that night the *Missouri* was headed for Sasebo, where she replenished fuel and ammunition while Admiral Smith shifted his flag to the destroyer tender *Dixie*. Within 24 hours the *Missouri* was under way again, headed for Inchon.

---

1. Generally speaking, the greater the calibre of the naval gun, the greater its effectiveness upon enemy targets at the front line. If further proof was needed, the 16-inch guns of the *Iowa*, *Missouri*, *Wisconsin* and *New Jersey* demonstrated that pound for pound they were the most efficient rifles in the Korean War. **The Sea War in Korea**, Cagle & Marson, U. S. Naval Institute.

U.S. CRUISER **MANCHESTER** was a sturdy fleet-mate of **MIGHTY MO** in Korean waters.

Escorted by destroyer *Mansfield,* she reached the invasion area at midday on September 20 and began artillery support of the United States Army's Seventh Infantry Division. The Hampton Roads humiliation of *Mighty Mo* hadn't been forgotten. Upon joining the assault forces of Inchon, the cruiser *Toledo* signalled "Found a mudbank to sit on, Mac?" Undaunted, *Missouri* replied, "Go home, small fry. We brought the real guns."

Ironically enough, *Mighty Mo* did find a mud bank to sit on at Inchon. When her bombardment anchorage position was assigned by Captain J. R. Topper, Seventh Fleet Service Forces commander, Captain Duke checked the chart and told Topper "with the bearings you gave me I'll be on the mud at low tide!" But that was the idea. The deliberate grounding gave *Missouri* a five to seven degree port list

and increased her guns' range by a good five miles.

The next afternoon, General of the Army Douglas MacArthur returned to the *Missouri* for the first time since the signing of the Japanese surrender five years before. On this visit he was accompanied by Vice Admiral A. D. Struble, Seventh Fleet commander, Major General E. M. Almond, U. S. Army X Corps commander, and other flag and general officers. *Missouri's* war diary records that, "General MacArthur expressed his pleasure and satisfaction in revisiting the scene of his acceptance of the surrender of Japan in World War II." Admiral Struble, who was in command of naval operations at Inchon, recalls the visit well and has provided these notes:

"MacArthur visited *Missouri* during Inchon. I met him with my barge and took him down the

THROUGH THE NIGHT of December 5, 1950, the port city of Chinnampo was a wall of flame as United Nations demolition teams and naval ships set fire to military installations after the last U. N. ground forces and refugees had been safely removed.

SMOKE RISES from the North Korean port of Chinnampo, as military targets are blown up following evacuation of United Nations troops and Korean refugees.

LANDING SHIPS unloading at Yellow Beach, Wonsan, Korea . . . October, 1950.

A CHEERING SIGHT from one of **MISSOURI'S** helicopters in October, 1950 was this column of North Korean prisoners crossing the air-strip near Yellow Beach.

MINESWEEPER AT WORK in Wonsan harbor; U.S. Cruiser **ST. PAUL** in the background.

channel to the *M.* where he was received with side honors and his flag hoisted. We toured the ship briefly, including seeing the Surrender Plaque, and then sat in the captain's cabin and had quite a discussion of the current problem, etc. As I am sure you know, we had anchored *M.* where her gunfire would cover a part of the road from Suwon to Seoul and could fire at night when our aviation could not cover the road. I believe the *M.* was able to cover a stretch of the road about three miles long."

That night General Almond established his headquarters ashore in the city of Inchon, and on the 29th Captain Duke participated in the triumphal march into Seoul, where General MacArthur formally restored its Capitol to the Republic of Korea.

The rest of *Missouri's* service in Korean waters was as a part of the carrier task force off the eastern coast of Korea in the Sea of Japan, and as flagship for the Seventh Fleet commander. Shortly after receiving Admiral Struble's flag at Sasebo on October 7, she headed a United Nations bombardment force against the North Korean port cities of Chongjin and Tanchon. Then she served as task force flagship during the amphibious landings at Wonsan in October. During November and December she cruised with the carrier force, but on December 23 she was called upon again to deliver broadsides ashore in support of the redeployment of X Corps from Hungnam. With the North Korean invasion armies completely broken, Red China had thrown her massive land forces into the fray. By late November, the First Marine Division, which had been advancing north al-

most without opposition, found itself under the massed, fanatical attack of six Chinese divisions. Similar odds were soon being faced by other United Nations forces ashore, and an orderly withdrawal began toward the 38th Parallel. It was decided to evacuate the troops as they had arrived . . . by sea . . . and the ports of Inchon, Chinnampo, Wonsan and Hungnam were all successfully used for this purpose.[2]

While friendly troops were evacuated from the beach, *Missouri's* main battery sent 68 rounds crashing into the enemy command post and troop areas, her spotting plane estimating 400 troops and 20 buildings destroyed. On Christmas eve she gave the communists a parting gift of 94 16-inch and 302 five-inch high explosive rounds. The amphibious rescue operation was completed by four o'clock that afternoon, thus bringing to a close 52 consecutive

---

2. The retreat from the Yalu did not give communist forces undisputed control of all areas north of the 38th Parallel. Admiral Smith selected several places above the United Nations battle line to hold with the blockading force. Anticipating the eventual return of our armies, one of the positions was Wonsan; and thus began the siege of Wonsan, designed to make it useless as a base of operations for the enemy. The control of the ships over this vital port and its communications always posed the threat of another amphibious landing 100 miles above the battle line and in the communists' rear. General Ridgeway heartily endorsed the siege, which lasted three years and continued to restrict enemy operations. On March 19, *Missouri* became the first battleship to participate in the siege, blasting enemy gun positions with her 16-inch fire.

WONSAN SMOLDERS, as a British destroyer of Task Force 95, left, prowls close to shore in search of new targets.

FIRE IN THE NIGHT off Hungnam, Korea in December, 1950 as United Nations troops were evacuated from the beaches after massive Red Chinese counterattack was described in routine language
of **MISSOURI'S** war diary for December 23 . . . "At 0031 anchored off HUNGNAM, KOREA, 1,000
yards to seaward of swept channel buoy No. 9. At 1230I **MISSOURI** went to General Quarters. Commenced firing the main battery (turret II) at 1320I. Targets were troop bivouac areas, command post
in HAMHUNG, and artillery concentrations. Spotting was conducted by naval aircraft. Ceased fire
at 1605I, firing missions complete. Spotting plane estimated 400 troops and 20 buildings destroyed.
* * * At 1904I 3 LSMR's bombarded shore with 5-inch rockets. At 2000I commenced main and secondary battery harassing and interdiction fire missions on designated targets in the vicinity of
HUNGNAM defense perimiter." The forward 16-inch guns of **MIGHTY MO** were pictured in action
in this dramatic night photograph, while further insore the rocket ships trace a deadly pattern against
the sky. The Hungnam amphibious operation was successfully completed the following evening,
Christmas Eve.

SIEGE GUNS ROAR as the United Nations Blockading and Escort Force (TF 95) sent an average of at least one high explosive shell per minute screaming toward the communist-held North Korean port of Wonsan. These are the six-inch batteries of cruiser

days of sustained combat operations by *Mighty Mo*.[3]

Late in January, 1951, *Missouri* struck against Kansong, Kosong and Kangnung on the east coast of Korea, then dashed around the peninsula to assist advancing Eighth Army troops in the Inchon area. With this city secured, she returned to the east coast and

3. *"Missouri* began main battery fire on 23 December at road targets between Ori-ri and Hungnam. 'Though we didn't really need her firepower' said (Rear Admiral J. H.) Doyle (commander, Amphibious Forces), 'General Almond kept suggesting that we call in the *Missouri*. So I called for her and gave her a target selection. She quickly got a hit on an enemy troop shelter, and the air spotter reported that the Chinese Communists were running out in all directions.' In addition to her main battery fire, *Missouri's* five-inch batteries contributed harassing and illumination fire in covering the withdrawal of the last ground elements." **The Sea War in Korea,** Commander Malcolm W. Cagle, U. S. N., and Commander Frank A. Manson, U. S. N., United States Naval Institute, 1957.

COSMOPOLITAN NATURE OF U. N. BLOCKADING AND ESCORT FORCE is typified by this conference between Admiral Smith and Capitan de Corbeta (Lieutenant Commander) J. C. Reyes Canal of the Colombian Navy, commander of the A.R.C. **ALMIRANTE PADILLA.**

MANNING THE SIDE, side boys and ship's bos'n pipe General Douglas MacArthur aboard U.S.S. **MISSOURI** for conference with Admiral Struble.

GENERAL MacARTHUR, center, with Admiral Struble, left, and Commander McBain, in flag cabin of **MISSOURI** at Inchon in September, 1950.

"AT 13251 ON 21 SEPTEMBER, General of the Army Douglas MacArthur (CinCFE) accompanied by Vice Admiral A. D. Struble, USN (CJTF 7), Major General E. M. Almond (CG X Corps), and other subordinate commanders made an official call on the Commanding Officer MISSOURI. General MacArthur expressed his pleasure and satisfaction in revisiting the scene of his acceptance of the surrender of Japan in World War II. He and his party left the ship at 13561" . . . *War Diary, U.S.S. MISSOURI, 1950.* MacArthur is shown below being welcomed aboard by Captain Duke.

the combat zone on March 11 for a final five days of bombarding enemy bridges and rail centers at Chongjin, Chaho and Wonsan. Then on March 28, having been relieved by her sister ship *New Jersey,* she headed home . . . for Long Beach, California. Admiral Struble remained aboard, having been reassigned to command the First Fleet. She arrived there on April 12, 1951, to a tumultuous welcome, and two days later departed for Norfolk via the Panama Canal.

From the time of her departure from Norfolk on August 19, 1950, until her return on April 27, 1951, *Mighty Mo* had steamed 62,100 miles. During her combat operations in Korean waters she had fired 2,895 16-inch and 8,043 five-inch projectiles with a total weight of well over three thousand tons.

And few of the American, Republic of Korea and United Nations fighting men whom she had protected and supported would agree that

HISTORY REPEATS ITSELF as General Douglas MacArthur, with Admiral Struble and Captain Duke, watches his five-starred flag climb to the yardarm of the **MISSOURI** at Inchon in September, 1950. It had last flown on **MIGHTY MO** in Tokyo Bay on September 2, 1945.

shelled the vital rail centers of Tanchon and Songjin, above the 38th Parallel. Between missions she anchored at Pusan with other units of the Pacific Fleet and United Nations forces, and was visited by President and Mrs. Syngman Rhee, U. S. Ambassador to Korea J. Muccio, Rear Admiral Sohn, chief of staff of the ROK Navy, the president of the National Assembly, the minister of National Defense, Army General Garvin, and Admirals Smith and I. N. Kiland. A few days later the ship's side was manned again to welcome another distinguished visitor, Lieutenant General Matthew B. Ridgeway, commanding general of the Eighth Army, who came aboard by helicopter for an official call on Admiral Struble.

On the first day of March, *Missouri* reached Yokosuka, Japan, for a two-week upkeep period. Next morning Captain Duke assembled the ship's company to present commendations to 229 men, and to say goodby. He was relieved by Captain G. C. Wright, who took her back to

ON THE SHINING SURRENDER DECK, Mrs. Douglas Mac-Arthur is shown the Surrender Plaque by Vice Admiral Struble, Seventh Fleet commander, at Yokosuka, Japan in March, 1951. The condition of the historic quarterdeck of the commissioned **MISSOURI** is in marked contrast to its present neglected state. (See photographs page 148.)

there is no place for a battleship in the atomic age.

The Kansas City *Star,* admittedly a bit prejudiced in favor of U.S.S. *Missouri,* published the following editorial during her Korean war service:

"THE COMEBACK OF THE 'MIGHTY MO'

"Let every loyal son of Missouri hold his head high and his chest thrust forward. The proud battleship named for this state has redeemed herself.

"It was a dark and perverse day last January 17 when the Big Mo found herself stuck on a Chesapeake Bay mudbank, as helpless as a fish beached by the tide. Before fourteen tugs could huff and puff the *Missouri* to floating safety, she had become a pathetic figure of ridicule, a national joke for all her gallant past.

"Whereupon the Navy, in its embarrassment, relegated the grand lady warrior to the rocking chair status of a training ship. In an era when atomic weapons would be all-determining, the *Missouri* was supposed to be as obsolete as a wooden frigate.

"So what happens? Along comes the Korean War and the admirals find a job made to order for their only active battlewagon. The *Missouri* hears the call to arms, glides out of semi-retirement and heads for the scenes of conflict.

"While racing eleven thousand miles she cuts through a hurricane, eludes a tropical storm and arrives off the Korean coast with a typhoon lashing its tail behind her. Then the queen of the seas stands near the Communist-occupied port of Samchok while her sixteen-inch guns soften defenses for the United States Marines and infantry landing in the first big United Nations counterattack of the war.

"It's the sweetest vindication possible for a fighting lady. And there can be no true Missourian so lacking in sentiment as not to be aboard his state's favorite vessel in spirit as she goes about the grim business of gaining new and greater glory."

AT BATTLE STATION in Korean waters.

SIXTEEN-INCH SALVOS light the night sky off Korea as they send destruction rumbling toward communist invaders.

KOREAN COMBAT COMMANDERS discuss naval operations aboard the flagship of the Blockading and Escort Force. Left to right, Vice Admiral William G. Andrewes, commander British Commonwealth Naval Forces in Korea waters; Vice Admiral Arthur D. Struble, commander U.S. Seventh Fleet; Rear Admiral Allan E. Smith, commander United Nations Blockading and Escort Force.

U.S.S. MISSOURI firing at shore targets, Wonsan. March, 1951.

Part of the United Nations fleet at anchor, Sasebo, Japan, November, 1950. Ships include British aircraft repair carrier **UNICORN,** foreground, cruiser **JUNEAU,** carriers **VALLEY FORGE** and **PRINCETON** and various auxiliary vessels. (opposite page)

U.S.S. **PRINCETON,** a unit of the Fast Carrier Force in Korean
waters, prepares to launch Corsair and Panther jet fighters
against communist-held positions in Korea.

H.M.S. **THESEUS,** 13,350-ton British light fleet aircraft carrier,
was another unit of United Nations sea forces off Korea. Here
she's obviously all gussied up to have her picture taken, the crew
in formation to spell out her name forward, and her planes neatly but unfunctionally lined up aft.

MIGHTY MO FIRES A SALVO. Note one premature shell burst and five other shells in flight.

THANKSGIVING DAY, 1950 found **MIGHTY MO** steaming with elements of Task Force 77 to the eastward of Wonsan. Her war diary reported, "At 07331 MISSOURI went alongside CACAPON for fueling and cleared at 11251, having received 274,158 gallons of fuel oil." The fleet oiler is pictured here in blustery seas with fueling line made fast to the **MISSOURI.**

DEADLY SILHOUETTES of naval guns point toward the devastation they have dealt to communist shore installations in Korea.

ROK PRESIDENT SYNGMAN RHEE presents the Republic of Korea medal to Admiral Smith for his leadership in coordinating United Nations ships on patrol, bombardment and siege missions off the war-torn peninsula.

COMMUNIST-CAMOUFLAGED buildings near Wonsan. October, 1950.

AMERICAN MEDAL FOR A KOREAN NAVAL HERO. Admiral Smith decorates a ROK sailor at South Korean Naval Academy.

ANOTHER BRONZE STAR MEDAL is awarded to a ROK naval captain at the Korean Naval Academy ceremony.

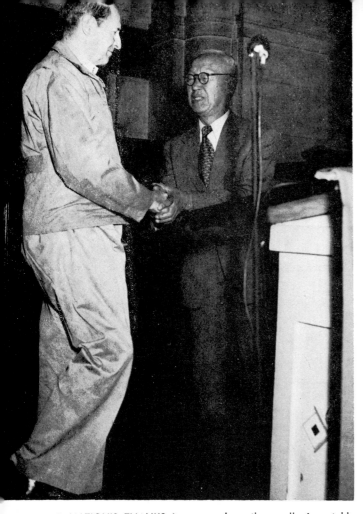

NATIONAL ENSIGN OF THE REPUBLIC OF KOREA flies from the mainmast of **MISSOURI** in honor of President Rhee's visit.

A NATION'S THANKS is expressed on the usually inscrutable face of ROK President Singman Rhee at conclusion of ceremonies in Seoul on September 29, 1950, when General MacArthur returned the capitol to the rightful government.

PRESIDENT RHEE, Vice Admiral Struble and Madame Rhee inspect the helicopter on the after deck of **MISSOURI.** During the second World War the battleship carried twin seaplanes, but these were replaced by the more versatile choppers during the Korean War.

AT THE STARBOARD GANGWAY President Singman Rhee of the Republic of Korea boards **MIGHTY MO** to visit U.S. Seventh Fleet commander, Vice Admiral Struble.

PRESIDENT SYNGMAN RHEE and Rear Admiral Won Yil Sohn, Chief of ROK Naval Operations, pass through honor guard of South Korean Navy side boys at South Korean Naval Academy near Chinhae. The ROK President visited the academy for an awards ceremony during which Rear Admiral Allan E. Smith, commander of the United Nations Blockading and Escort Force, decorated ROK naval personnel with United States Silver and Bronze Star medals.

LAND AND SEA COMMANDERS meet on the deck of the MIS-SOURI at Inchon in February, 1951, as Captain Duke, Admiral Struble and other officers of the Seventh Fleet flagship welcome General Matthew Ridgeway, commander of United Nations ground forces in Korea.

THERE'S ALWAYS HOPE, regardless of how far from home a military unit may roam. The ubiquitous comedian is pictured entertaining the men of **MIGHTY MO** off Wonsan in October, 1950.

IN **MISSOURI'S** FLAG CABIN, Bob Hope explains naval strategy to Seventh Fleet Commander Struble.

MIGHTY MO CRUISES the coast of North Korea.

ALOHA TO A GALLANT LADY. Framed by Hawaiian palms, **MIGHTY MO** glides through Pearl Harbor on her way back to the United States, having been relieved of Korean fighting duties by her sister ship, **NEW JERSEY.**

Chapter Nine

"Sweep —
For Humanity's Sake
— Sweep"

TASK FORCE 95 . . . the United Nations Blockading and Escort Force . . . of which U.S.S. *Missouri* was, for a time, flagship, had apparent full control of the sea around Korea, and Seventh Fleet controlled the air above it. This had permitted the amphibious landings at Inchon which had broken up the North Korean army. The landings at Wonsan, a month later, were to be the knockout punch.

Aware that Wonsan lies only 400 miles south and west of the major Russian naval base of Vladivostok, allied commanders were acutely aware of the possibility of Soviet naval and air intervention. As Admiral Smith's Task Force 95 approached Wonsan . . . its job to escort transports jammed with 50,000 American soldiers and marines safely into Wonsan harbor . . . it was fully prepared to deal with any Soviet submarine or aerial attack.

So an urgent message dispatched by Admiral Smith aroused shocked disbelief from Seventh Fleet headquarters to the Pentagon. The message began: *"The United States Navy has lost command of the sea in Korean waters."*

What had stopped this mighty eleven-nation sea and air force in its tracks? The answer could be summed up in two words . . . Russian mines. The Wonsan invasion fleet ran into something no one had prepared for . . . a massive field of more than 3,000 mines, laid in secrecy under the direction of Russian naval experts.

In his report to higher headquarters, Admiral Smith told it like it was: "At Wonsan, with a maximum of ten days allowed for mine sweeping, it required 16 days to get into the Blue-

Yellow beaches. In the six extra days our large amphibious force with 50,000 troops went around in circles; our comparative armada of carriers and aircraft circled; all waiting with the spotlight on six small wooden ships (one of which broke down) struggling to clear the way to the beaches . . . As it was, there has been some talk of the delay in landing being the cause of the Chinese divisions gaining positions in North Korea. If the Korean campaign had depended upon the time factor in landing at Wonsan, a failure might have resulted and the Navy would have been blamed."

The late Admiral Forrest P. Sherman, then Chief of Naval Operations, agreed with Smith's summation in an interview with George Fielding Eliot, later published in *Collier's* magazine in 1953:

"Let's admit it," Admiral Sherman told Eliot, "They caught us with our pants down. Those damned mines cost us eight days delay in getting the troops ashore, and more than 200 casualties. That's bad enough. But I can all too easily think of circumstances when eight days delay offshore could mean losing a war.

"Hoke's right; when you can't go where you want to when you want to, you haven't got command of the sea. And command of the sea is the rock-bottom foundation of all our war plans. We've been plenty submarine-conscious and air-conscious. Now we're going to start getting mine-conscious . . . beginning last week."

The Wonsan mines were a badly needed reminder that this sort of underwater warfare has always been a favorite weapon of the Soviet Navy, and a successful one. As Admiral

GALLANT SHIPS OF WONSAN were the small minesweepers which opened the approaches of the harbor to the United Nations fleet. Two of them are shown here at their dangerous work off Yellow Beach.

STRAIN OF WONSAN MINESWEEPING OPERATIONS is pictured on the face of Admiral Smith, right, and Lt. Commander D. V. "Dusty" Shouldice, Commander Mine Squadron Three, aboard the squadron flagship PLEDGE. Shouldice earned the Navy Cross for his actions during the Wonson sweeping operations; PLEDGE was one of the several minesweepers lost during that hectic period.

EXECUTIVE OFFICER Bruce Barrington of the minesweeper PARTRIDGE is rescued amid floating debris after his ship struck a floating mine while sweeping off Yong-yang, southeast of Wonsan, and sank in less than ten minutes. Eight others of her crew were killed. PARTRIDGE was the last of four American minesweepers lost during the Korean war.

DEATH AT WONSAN. The ROK minesweeper **YMS 516** explodes in a geyser of flame, water and debris after striking a Russian contact mine and sinking with heavy losses.

Smith pointed out, "History shows that navies 'hang on' to the instruments that have been most successful, even though other weapons eventually displace them."

The dramatic if temporary success of the Russian mine fields at Wonsan had a lasting impact on United States Navy planning. Ever since Wonsan, mine warfare has been accepted as a fact of life. During the two years of the Korean War, seventy percent of all naval casualties afloat were caused by mines. And the mine sweeper crews, comprising only two percent of naval forces in the Far East, suffered 35 percent of all the Navy's casualties in that war.

Wonsan brought mine warfare training back to the United States Navy and so was, perhaps, a blessing in disguise, but at the time it brought only headaches to the man responsible for getting the troops ashore and the supply lines established to maintain them.

One of the expedients used by him to solve the problem resulted in a comic opera sortie by a fleet of Japanese mine sweepers. The story is told, in his own words, by the man most closely involved in it, Vice Admiral Allan E. Smith:

"Inchon had been won. Now, October 1950, fifty thousand U. S. Marine and Army troops were at sea in the Amphibious Force enroute from Inchon to make a landing on Wonsan Green and Yellow Beaches. . . . And there we were, in the approaches to Wonsan with six small wooden minesweepers, and only seven days remaining before (L) Landing Day.

"Our sweepers had cleared a channel from the hundred fathom mark to our present position on the thirty fathom mark, a 12 mile stretch. We had paid a terrific price. Our two larger steel sweepers had been sunk by enemy gunfire and mines; and many of their gallant crews had been lost. There remained to complete a swept channel to the Green and Yellow Beaches, seven long and dangerous miles.

"Wonsan Bay, from seaward, has the shape of an old fashioned keyhole; a wide 'V' ap-

MISSOURI AT ANCHOR OFF WONSAN is approached by destroyer (above) which will take Admiral Struble to inner harbor to observe progress of minesweeping. Admiral Struble is shown (below) aboard the Canadian destroyer **ATHABASCA,** en route to the sweeping area. With him are Lt. Commander Peacock and Commander Welland, RCN, of the **ATHABASCA.**

proach; a squeezed in waist; then expanding rapidly into a large eight mile circle, across to the City of Wonsan with its sandy beaches.

"On that cold October day, I knew that between us and the beaches lay several thousand anchored contact mines, and worse, and more deadly, in the shallower waters on the bottom, lay magnetic mines. These were Russian mines and good ones, for the Russian Navy has an impressive record of successful mine warfare; as the Russian Army has of successful artillery and rocket victories. The number of mines, the pressure of time, the bitter north wind, the choppy sea, the sporadic firing by the enemy from the islands in the bay, the very, very slow process of sweeping magnetic mines, and our exhausted crews; all these spoke up to demand a drastic change in the situation, if I was to succeed in meeting (L) day.

"I probed the minds of the staff, but found no new ideas; though I did find hard determination there. And then that Napoleonic recollection struck me. Yes, that was it; those Japanese minesweepers, still sweeping the Inland Sea for the mines planted there by our Army Air Corps and Navy in World War II. Those Japanese sweepers could help; they could help, if I could get them.

"Off went an urgent dispatch to Admiral Joy in Tokyo, Commander of U. S. Naval Forces in the Far East, information to General Mac-

Arthur, requesting some Japanese sweepers in this urgent situation. The tedious time consuming sweeping operations continued with no reply from Tokyo; but at the third morning twilight, five Japanese minesweepers and their mother ship were led in from seaward by our guard ship; and were soon nested alongside of each other at a mooring buoy we had anchored five hundred yards from my temporary destroyer flagship. The Japanese civilian in charge, Mr. Tamara, came aboard to inform me that they were all under contract to the Japanese Government; that the masters of the sweepers understood English, and that they were ready to sweep mines. The briefing of Mr. Tamara and the masters of his ships began, covering all phases of the sweeping operations by oral and written instructions and by furnishing accurate colored charts showing areas swept; those to be swept, prohibited areas, and the section assigned to be swept by the Japanese. To complete the briefing, all lay up on the bridge to see for themselves the buoys marking the various areas as shown on the charts. Everyone satisfied, Mr. Tamara and his sweepers were soon underway and sweeping; but in late afternoon, one of the Japanese sweepers managed to cross into a prohibited area, hit a mine, blew up and disappeared. All were rescued except one Japanese, who was never sighted after the explosion. The Japanese ships had remote control to their engines, which accounts for the small loss of life. It would have been greater in our sweepers, as ours were not equipped with remote control of the engines. Nevertheless, sweeping continued until dark, and observations from the bridge and over the telephone confirmed satisfactory progress.

"As twilight shaded into darkness, one by one the small sweepers nestled alongside their mother ship for the night and began preparations for the next day's sweep. The captains reported aboard the flagship with their detailed data which the staff correlated; analyzed and wrote out the next day's instructions. By 3 a.m., all was ready for the morning twilight start of operations. I turned in, but was awakened at 6 a.m. by one of the staff speaking through the tired air, 'The Japanese say they want to sweep where there are no mines.' 'Ridiculous,' I thought, 'I must be dreaming.' But no, it was repeated, and I was sitting up. 'Well, send for Mr. Tamara, at once' was my reaction. In fifteen minutes, Mr. Tamara and I were fac-

THE HORNED DEATH BELOW . . . a floating Russian mine off Wonsan. October, 1950.

ing each other in the destroyer's small chart room.

"Without preliminaries, I began, 'Mr. Tamara, what is the difficulty?'

"Mr. Tamara, five feet five, broad in the beam, serious, hissed and bowed from the waist. 'Yes,' he replied, 'men want sweep where no mines.'

" ' Well,' I answered brusquely, 'yours is not a good reason, and I will tell you why.' And then and there I began and completed an oration on the historical struggle of the people of the United States of America in their fight for the freedom of the individual; the fight for humanity itself.

135

" 'Mr. Tamara,' I continued, 'almost two centuries ago, we Americans fought the British to free outselves from domination, from unfair taxes; a war fought for a better life for the individual.'

"Mr. Tamara hissed and bowed from the waist.

" 'Then we fought the French in an undeclared war, because they began to oppress us.'

"Mr. Tamara hissed and bowed.

" 'In 1812 we fought the British again to stop them from impressing our seamen. Do you understand, Mr. Tamara?'

"Mr. Tamara understood, hissed and bowed from the waist.

" 'In mid-century we fought the Mexicans.' I hesitated and let the Mexican War go without further comment.

"Anyway Mr. Tamara hissed and bowed, as I hurried along.

" 'Then the Americans in North United States fought the South, for the freedom of the individual; for humanity's sake. Do you follow me?'

"Mr. Tamara followed; hissed and bowed.

" 'In 1917, we entered World War I to fight the Germans, and in that war Japan fought on our side. We were fighting for the individual's rights; to make the world safe for Democracy.'

"Mr. Tamara's eyes rounded, as he hissed and bowed.

" 'Then came World War II, and in that war we fought both the Germans and the Japanese. We knew we were fighting for freedom and for the individual. You know that is right, Mr. Tamara.'

"But Mr. Tamara had already drawn himself up to five feet seven, and announced, 'Yes, I was an officer in the Japanese Imperial Navy.'

"I continued quickly. 'Now here we are again, this time in Korea, fighting for the individual, for freedom, for all humanity. Cannot you, Mr. Tamara, tell your crews all that I have said and that we are fighting for the Japanese too, each of them. Those are the reasons why your crews should sweep where we want them to sweep; and they will be doing their part to win this war for freedom, when they sweep as I have directed; otherwise they might as well be back in Japan. Do you understand, Mr. Tamara?'

"Mr. Tamara understood, gave a last hiss and a last bend at the waist. As I opened the door to let him out, I added in a firm and commanding voice, 'Mr. Tamara, you have exactly twenty minutes to inform your crews and to get underway and start sweeping where your instructions and charts state.' I glanced at my watch and Mr. Tamara departed with a quick step.

"In the next fifteen minutes, I reviewed our plans of the day, and assured myself that the Japanese were assigned a task well within their capabilities. Then I went topside to the bridge. The bay was white capped as usual. Inshore were our six tiny sweepers in good tactical formation, but almost motionless as they towed their heavy gear across the bay. Beyond our tiny sweepers, now but a few miles were the graceful curving white beaches of Wonsan. The city was framed by rolling green hills, all crowned by the distant snow-capped mountains.

"At any other time, this dramatic view would have stayed me; but I swung around to the port side, raised my binoculars to the Japanese sweeper nest. I could see Mr. Tamara, standing above the crews gathered around him; and as he was gesturing, the sun broke through, warming the entire scene and the situation. I glanced at my watch; nineteen minutes and the Japanese crews were dispersing and hopping over to their own craft. Twenty minutes now; and, yes; the Japanese were casting off. First, the leader, then the second sweeper, the third, the fourth, and last, the mother ship, all in the manner of well ordered ships. They formed column with regular intervals between the sweepers, steamed past me on the port side of the destroyer.

"Then the column turned right ninety degrees; then the column made another ninety degree turn toward the channel we had swept in from seaward, and the Japanese sweepers kept right on steaming five hundred miles back to Japan!

"Soon I dispatched another message to Admiral Joy, information to General MacArthur; stating that if they would insure that the Japanese were not paid and were never permitted to go to sea again; then I, as long as I lived, would never again make another speech in the cause of freedom, or for humanity's sake."

PRESIDENT AND MRS. RHEE, on visit to U.S. Seventh Fleet flagship, join Admiral Struble for a snack in **MISSOURI'S** crews' mess.

South Korean gunboat strikes a mine.

Chapter Ten

Mighty Even In Mothballs

ITH U.S.S. *New Jersey* replacing her in Korean waters, *Missouri* r e t u r n e d quickly to peacetime routine. Within little more than a month from her arrival at Norfolk, on June 4, 1951, she embarked nearly eight hundred Academy and R.O.T.C. midshipmen. As flagship for the 1951 Midshipmen Practice Squadron and for Commander Cruiser Force, U.S. Atlantic Fleet, Rear Admiral James L. Holloway, Jr., she made good will calls at Oslo, Norway and Cherbourg, France, before culminating the training phase of the cruise with gunnery exercises off Guantanamo.

On August 3, *Missouri* again sailed from Norfolk on her second midshipman training cruise, this time with 765 Naval R.O.T.C. students. Scheduled ports of call were New York and Colon, Panama Canal Zone.

When the cruise was completed in September, *Mighty Mo* went into drydock at Norfolk for another major overhaul and upkeep period, during which Captain Wright was relieved by Captain John Sylvester. On January 31, 1952, she sailed to Guantanamo Bay again for six weeks of rigorous operational training, protecting herself against simulated air and surface raids and atomic attack, and sharpening her offensive teeth in antiaircraft and shore bombardment missions.

Ready for any mission and with the flag of Rear Admiral H. R. Thurber, Commander Battleship Division Two, flying at her yardarm, *Mighty Mo* arrived back in Norfolk in mid-March.

But there were no more combat missions for *Missouri*. She contined to train midshipmen, reservists and regular Navy personnel during 1952 and 1953, but with the end of active hostilities in Korea came another round of defense cutbacks. By 1954 the word was out . . . *Mighty Mo* was headed for retirement.

In mid-September, 1954, the *Missouri* steamed majestically up the Northwest coast of the United States and swung to starboard past Tatoosh Island and the rocky headland of Cape Flattery. Off Port Angeles, Washington, she paused to pick up a Puget Sound pilot; then moved slowly up the Sound to a berth at Naval Pier 91 in Seattle.

People were aware that *Mighty Mo* was going to leave the high seas. During a short open house on the afternoon of her arrival at Seattle, more than five thousand people came to pay their respects to her.

The morning of February 26, 1955, dawned gray and windy on Puget Sound. The Naval Shipyard at Bremerton, across the bay from Seattle, was swept by cold rain and squalls of wet snow. It was the morning of *Missouri's* decommissioning, and it was in gloomy contrast to the bright day more than a decade earlier when her commission pennant had first risen to her yard arm. Only a small group was there for the ceremony of her retirement, and the miserable weather drove them from the open quarterdeck to the wardroom. The only figure on the deck of the *Missouri* as she left the active Fleet was that of Seaman Carl Dewese, who stood at the stern in the shelter of the aircraft crane to haul her ensign down.

Five months later, as the tenth anniversary of the Japanese surrender approached, Richard Nokes of the Portland *Oregonian,* wrote this account of the ship where the last act of the bloody drama had been played out:

"The U.S.S. *Missouri,* her 16-inch rifles sealed and her engines partially dismantled, slumbers in semi-obscurity, the flagship of the mothball fleet in Puget Sound, as the tenth anniversary of her greatest hour draws near.

"Ten years ago this Friday, September 2, was surrender day—the end of World War II,

BON VIVANTS. Annapolis and R.O.T.C. midshipmen on shore leave savour the charm of a classic French sidewalk cafe.

DID YOU MEET ANY NICE GIRLS WHILE YOU WERE IN PARIS? Midshipmen of the Cherbourg training cruise appraise the ageless charms of the Venus de Milo at the Louvre.

the date the Japanese officially gave up the struggle against just such weapons of war as the *Mighty Mo* and her 2700 fighting sailors.

"Millions of men had died and millions others had bled to make possible that historic moment in which the chief of staff of the army and the foreign minister of Japan came aboard the Missouri and gravely scratched their signatures to a document that ended the world's greatest conflict.

"The Mo played her part in that war. Her keel was laid at Brooklyn navy yard June 6, 1941, six months before the Japanese attacked Pearl Harbor. She was launched January 28, 1944, and a not-yet-famous senator from Missouri, Harry S. Truman, called her 'the greatest warship of all time.'

"The 58,000-ton giant was commissioned in July and later that year joined the Pacific fleet. Japan already was doomed but nobody knew it.

"The *Missouri* joined Admiral Marc Mitscher's fast carrier task force 58 in the first mass air strikes against Japan February 16 and 17. Her guns first barked in anger February 19 off Iwo Jima, and she drew her first blood that same day when the ship's five-inch guns brought down a Japanese plane.

"After the bloody Iwo landing, she escorted Mitscher's carriers in air strikes against Tokyo itself.

"Then, on March 24, the *Missouri* with several other battleships began the bombardment of Okinawa. Her 16-inch rifles knocked out coastal defense installations, destroyed control towers, exploded an ammunition dump and destroyed and damaged large buildings.

"On April 11 she suffered her first wound when a low-flying kamikaze threaded its way through a wall of anti-aircraft fire and crashed against the starboard side aft. Gasoline and debris were thrown over the main deck. Fire broke out, but was quickly extinguished. The big ship never so much as altered her course. Five days later she came under suicide plane attack again, but none of the kamikazes could get through.

"But it was at the end of World War II that the *Missouri* had her great day of glory. Other ships had more valorous war records, but the *Mo* became the symbol of victory because she was designated by General Douglas MacArthur, supreme commander in the Pacific, as the site for the signing of the official surrender papers.

"Proudly the Missouri sailed into Tokyo bay in the wake of the minesweepers. Overhead roared 1200 carrier planes, around her were 380 other vessels big and small of the allied Pacific fleets.

"Aboard came 315 newspaper correspondents, cameramen and radio broadcasters of a dozen nations. It was the greatest press gathering of the war, possibly the greatest of all time. And the mothers, fathers, wives and sweethearts at home read every word of the story that unfolded on the *Mo*—a story that meant Johnny could come marching home, if he were still alive.

"On surrender day, September 2, at 0904 Tokyo time, the first of Japan's representatives affixed his signature. Four minutes later General MacArthur, Admiral Chester Nimitz and the highest ranking heroes of all the other allied nations signed their names.

"The great war was over.

"Today a bronze circle in the teakwood deck of the *Missouri* marks the spot where that largest war of all time ended. On a bulkhead near-by is another bronze plaque that bears the names of those who signed. In the quarters of Capt. K. F. Poehlmann of the Puget Sound reserve fleet hangs a copy of the surrender document.

"All New York turned out to welcome the *Mo* and her armada when they returned from Tokyo in October, 1945.

"Six months later the *Missouri* was sent to Istanbul, Turkey, bearing the body of Mehmet Munir Ertegun, Turkish ambassador to Washington. Before she came home, she visited Greece, Egypt, Italy, Algiers, Tangier, winning friends wherever she went.

"By 1949 the *Missouri* was the only American battleship left in active service. The rest were in mothballs, just as the *Mo* herself is today. Then in 1950 came the *Missouri's* and possibly the navy's most embarrassing hour. The big *Mo*, pride of the fleet, symbol of victory, the country's only battleship, got stuck in the mud in Chesapeake bay.

"As in everything else, the *Missouri* did a good job of it. She stuck fast for 15 days while tugs tugged, sailors lightened ship and admirals sweated.

"Finally she floated loose, and navy men everywhere again could face the world.

"But the *Missouri* was soon back on the glory road. She was the first American battleship to join in the Korean war in 1950. The *Missouri's* supremacy at bombarding shore installations and supply lines far inland with her one-ton shells was never contested by the enemy. In all, the *Mighty Mo* fired 7,600,000 pounds of shells at the Reds.

"A few months after the Korean war ended, the *Missouri* was ordered to the mothball fleet at Puget Sound naval shipyard, Bremerton.

"Like all other vessels before inactivation, she received a full overhaul, so in emergency she could be made ready for sea in the shortest possible time.

"She arrived in Puget Sound to a royal Seattle welcome September 15, 1954. On February 26, 1955, she was removed from the active fleet. But unlike the other ships in mothballs, the *Missouri* has not been decommissioned. She still proudly flies the national ensign and the jack. She is not entirely mothballed, either, for she is the mother ship of the Bremerton group of the reserve fleet, and aboard her live and

MIGHTY MUZZLE of **MISSOURI'S** center 16-inch gun in Turret Number One is protected by starred brass tampion. Interior of turrets and guns is protected by dehumidification.

. . . *photo by Judy Kay Wilson*

Portside view of **MISSOURI** "in mothballs" at Bremerton Navy Yard.

Visitors aboard the **MIGHTY MO** at Bremerton.
. . . *Washington State Dept. of Commerce &
Economic Development*

Sixteen-inch rifles.

. . . *photo by Judy Kay Wilson*

Reserve Fleet moorings, Bremerton.

. . . *photo by Judy Kay Wilson*

The authors visit the mothballed **MISSOURI.**

. . . *photo by Judy Kay Wilson*

work 600 sailors and officers who are the maintenance crew for the "fleet" at Bremerton.

"Her berthing and messing compartments, her galley, her offices are functioning. Her big wardroom, that once accommodated 200 officers, today serves 30. But the vitals that give a warship life—the bridge, the engines, the guns—are all secured and are under dehydration.

"For dehydration is the secret to the long-time preservation of America's fighting ships in reserve moorages on two oceans. Relative humidity is kept at 30 per cent through an intricate system of machines and installations. The dry air is piped into all possible spaces, through the ship's fire mains.

"Some of her machinery has been dismantled and coated with a thin-film preservative. Other machinery has just been opened to dry air. In some parts of the ship where dry air can't be piped, bags of silica gel, an absorbent, have been installed to remove moisture from the air.

"As far as possible, every article has been left in place. Every valve, fitting or electronic gismo that had to be disconnected was tagged so that in time of emergency activation teams would quickly know where it goes. Every spot from which equipment has been moved has been tagged indicating the exact location of that bit of gear.

"Most of the *Missouri's* below-deck spaces are sealed to make dehumidification possible. Even the great turrets and long gun barrels that once lobbed death at an enemy have been sealed and are protected by dry air. The Bremerton reserve group men keep a constant check on the *Missouri* and her sister battleships, such as the *West Virginia, Colorado, Maryland, Alabama,* the carrier *Bunker Hill* and a host of cruisers and amphibious vessels.

"Humidity gauges are visible in every cocoon. Sensing devices transmit a steady flow of readings to a central station indicating the percentage of moisture in remote dehydrated spaces. If the moisture content averages about 30 per cent, the dehydration machine goes into action.

"Everything exposed to the weather on the *Missouri* and her mothballed mates has been heavily painted or coated with a special preservative to keep out the rust, which could do far more damage than a kamikaze. The *Missouri's* hull is coated under water with a preservative. The hulls of some smaller ships are protected from rust electronically.

. . . AT REST IN QUIET WATERS
U.S.S. **MISSOURI** at reserve fleet mooring, Bremerton, Washington, 1969.

Five-inch gun turret.

. . . *photo by Judy Kay Wilson*

144

Forward superstructure framed by five-inch guns.
. . . photo by Judy Kay Wilson

Ship's bell, U.S.S. **MISSOURI**.
. . . photo by Judy Kay Wilson

"How soon could the *Missouri* be made ready for sea?

"In 30 days the *Mighty Mo* could go into action equipped just as she was in the Korean war. If she were to be modernized with new electronic equipment and new armament, an additional period in the navy yard would be required.

"Is mothballing a success?

"A tremendous success both from the economic and operational standpoints. The Missouri cost $100,000,000 to build at 1940 prices; she required three years from keel-laying to commissioning. Under mothballs, less than one per cent of the construction cost of a ship is spent on its maintenance. And a reserve ship can be made ready for sea in a month.

"The navy found out in the Korean war just how successful the mothball procedure had been. The carrier *Princeton,* for example, was put back into commission in 52 days, and this included full modernization. Just about half the ships that were put into the reserve fleet at Bremerton after World War II were pulled from beneath their bedcovers and sent into the Korean war. In no case did an activated ship suffer a breakdown.

"From the outside the *Mighty Mo* looks just like she did ten years ago when heroes trod her deck. Her lines are just as graceful, her guns are just as big.

"If America needs a ship to equip with atomic engines to display our peaceful atomic research projects in the far corners of the world, how about the *Mo?*

"A school child of any country would thrill to see this great ship, symbol of victory in the first war in which A-weapons were used; symbol of peace with her research exhibits aboard; reminder that he who takes up the sword shall perish by it."

Today, almost fifteen years after her relegation to the Navy's fleet of idle ships, U.S.S. *Missouri* still lies, majestic even in mothballs, at the Bremerton Navy Yard, ready as ever to steam again and to release her thunders upon the mighty deep, should she be needed.

Nor is *Mighty Mo* forgotten. Though Harry Truman once complained that the Navy had "stuck her away in a closet," thousands of visitors find their way to her each year, visit her, and leave her filled with awe for the great ship herself and for the sense of brave and historic events which she imparts.

Even if the time should come when, indeed, there is no practical place for a battleship, even in mothballs, it seems unlikely that *Mighty Mo* will make an ignominious last voyage to a scrapper's yard. For she is firmly enshrined in the hearts of all Americans, less as a symbol of war than of a just and humane peace.

Hopefully, our children's children will visit *Mighty Mo* and be reminded of all the things for which she stands.

After superstructure.

. . . *photo by Judy Kay Wilson*

A SOUVENIR OF YOUR VISIT TO THE
USS MISSOURI

Welcome Aboard

USS MISSOURI

LAUNCHED . . . . . JANUARY 29, 1944
COMMISSIONED . . . . JUNE 11, 1944
DECOMMISSIONED . FEBRUARY 26, 1955

U.S.S. MISSOURI

OVER THIS SPOT
ON 2 SEPTEMBER 1945
THE INSTRUMENT
OF FORMAL SURRENDER
OF JAPAN TO THE ALLIED POWERS
WAS SIGNED
THUS BRINGING TO A CLOSE
THE SECOND WORLD WAR.

THE SHIP AT THAT TIME
WAS AT ANCHOR
IN TOKYO BAY

LATITUDE 35°21'17" NORTH ~ LONGITUDE 139°45'36" EAST

13ND-NISMF BREM-5750/1 (Rev. 2-67)

147

EPILOG

ON APRIL 5, 1969, we revisited U.S.S. *Missouri* at Bremerton. Public attention that day was focused on the commissioning of a new ship, the fast combat support ship U.S.S. *Seattle*. The day was raw and showery, but even with these distractions, *Mighty Mo* was not forgotten. Probably a hundred visitors filed up her gangway while we were aboard. Many of them were children, to whom the great ship's glory days were only tales told by grandfathers or read in history books.

We talked to some of the children on the Surrender Deck and told them what had transpired there a quarter of a century ago. And a small boy looked up from the Surrender Plaque, its bronze damp from seeping rainwater and green with verdigris, and asked, "If it's important, why is it dirty?"

We had come aboard *Mighty Mo* expecting to feel proud, and a child's simple question made us feel ashamed.

The 600 men of the reserve unit have long since left the *Missouri* and there is no one to give her special care. Her interior, sealed and dehumidified, is being preserved, but outside, for the first time in her life, she is shabby and neglected. Dirt and flaked paint lay in the scuppers along the Surrender Deck. Careless workmen have dripped gray paint from the Number Two turret upon the once gleaming teakwood deck, and no one cared enough to have it cleaned up. The deck itself bore a sorry film of dirt and neglect, and is reached by a roughly-thrown-together wooden stairway more suitable for entering a warehouse than a national shrine.

The shining symbol of victory, of freedom and of justice shines no more. The deck where heroes trod is grimy as some abandoned tugboats. The bronze marker on the superstructure that lists their names is disfigured by the same clumsy painters who splashed the deck. There is nothing else to tell of what she did and what she stands for, save a framed chart of Tokyo Bay, propped haphazardly against the superstructure, and a posted reproduction of the surrender document. Four standards encircling the Surrender Plaque are connected by a chain painted with the look of cheap gilt.

Visitors on the Surrender Deck.

. . . *photo by Judy Kay Wilson*

149

It's hard to find the *Missouri* at her isolated mooring in Bremerton, but last year 185,000 Americans did find their way to this shabbiest of our national shrines and no doubt felt some sense of pride . . . or of shame . . . or perhaps a mixture of both.

If, as many claim, America has sunk into a poverty of spirit, *Missouri* is perhaps a fitting national monument. If not, something should be done to insure that, in the future, children will not come to her and ask . . . "If it's important, why is it dirty?"*

---

* Immediately following this depressing visit to *Missouri*, Admiral Smith wrote to Admiral Moorer, Chief of Naval Operations, pointing out the sad state of affairs aboard America's "Great and Wonderful Ship," and suggested these corrective measures:

To take advantage of this unique and invaluable public relations gift to the Navy, I suggest the following:

1. Request Congress to appropriate sufficient funds to maintain in clean, bright and proper condition, the "Surrender Deck". Such appropriation to be made under a title such as "National Memorials", and such appropriation to be entirely outside of Navy appropriations.
2. Include in the above, "The Captain's Country" as a museum which would have exhibits relating to the surrender, but more importantly, would display the meaning of seapower.
3. Organize and activate a program aboard the Missouri to inspire youth with an understanding of the security of our country and seapower.
4. Request the State of Washington to have mounted, large green directional signs every three blocks or so, from the Seattle Ferry to the Missouri moorage; a difficult journey at present. Probably ninety percent of the 185,000 tourists came by bus, since the Washington State Ferry System advertizes extensively, the visit to the Missouri. Otherwise, few tourists would know of the ship.
5. In the meantime, despite the lack of funds, get the bright work shined; scrape the paint off the deck; holly stone the deck; install an attractive and special ladder leading up the "Surrender Deck"; and generally convert the atmosphere into one of a shrine.
6. Alert the Navy League to the possibilities inherent in the Missouri.

POSTSCRIPT

CHIEF OF NAVAL OPERATIONS

13 MAY 1969

Dear Admiral Smith,

Many thanks for your letter with its excellent suggestions on how to improve the appearance of MISSOURI. We will promptly place some of them into effect. For example, plans for replacement of the ladder to the surrender deck are already underway.

In light of your helpful letter I intend to reexamine the problem to see what we can do to present the ship with proper dignity as a center of instruction and inspiration.

Thank you again for your most helpful interest and suggestions.

Sincerely,

T. H. Moorer

T. H. MOORER
Admiral, U. S. Navy

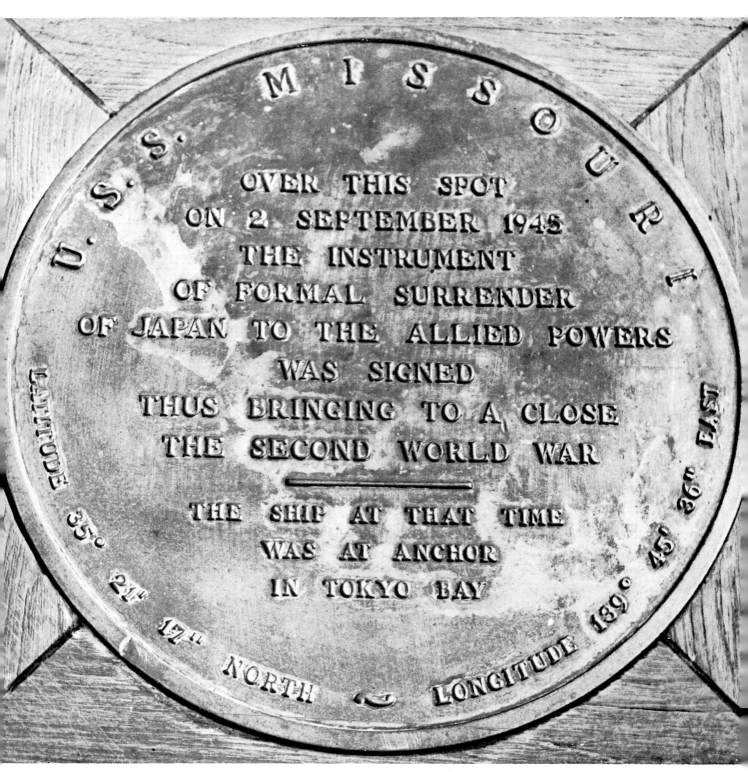

U.S.S. MISSOURI

OVER THIS SPOT
ON 2 SEPTEMBER 1945
THE INSTRUMENT
OF FORMAL SURRENDER
OF JAPAN TO THE ALLIED POWERS
WAS SIGNED
THUS BRINGING TO A CLOSE
THE SECOND WORLD WAR

———

THE SHIP AT THAT TIME
WAS AT ANCHOR
IN TOKYO BAY

LATITUDE 35° 21' 17" NORTH   LONGITUDE 139° 45' 36" EAST

THE PLAQUE, marking the sight of the formal ending of the second World War, has been viewed by hundreds of thousands of visitors in a score of ports. It is still a magnet which draws thousands of visitors to the mothballed **MISSOURI** each year.

FROM BOW TO STERN: The photograph above was taken from the extreme bow of the **MISSOURI** looking aft toward the forward superstructure and turrets and illustrates the upward sheer which helps give this class of battleships their graceful silhouette.

The view on the opposite page is taken from the stern, nearly nine hundred feet away, toward the after superstructure. The "cocoons" shown in both pictures protect the antiaircraft batteries and electronic gear.

. . . *photo by Judy Kay Wilson*

AFTER DECK of **MISSOURI** shows vast expanse of teakwood, once kept spotless by swabs and "holystones" of battleship's big crew, but now showing the effects of 14 years of layup.

. . . *photo by Judy Kay Wilson*

Starboard view of **MISSOURI** at Bremerton showing protective coverings over secondary batteries.

SEAL OF THE STATE OF MISSOURI decorates the Captain's Cabin aboard **MIGHTY MO.** Captain Callaghan during the shakedown cruise, is pictured wearing the "Ernie King" blue uniform, which was quickly discarded for less formal khakis when the ship entered the Pacific war zone.

CAPTAIN S. S. MURRAY, **MISSOURI'S** second commander, from May to November 1945.

CAPTAIN ROSCOE HILLENKOETTER, captain of the **MISSOURI** from November, 1945 to May, 1946.

ADMIRAL H. P. SMITH, pictured here in later years as Commander, Atlantic Fleet, was skipper of Missouri before and after her 1950 stranding.

CAPTAIN G. C. WRIGHT, **MISSOURI'S** skipper from March to October, 1951.

CAPTAIN I. T. DUKE, who commanded **MIGHTY MO** from April, 1950 to March, 1951.

U.S.S. MISSOURI

THE INSTRUMENT OF SURRENDER TERMINATING THE SECOND WORLD WAR
WAS SIGNED IN THIS SHIP, 2 SEPTEMBER 1945 EAST LONGITUDE DATE,
WHILE SHE LAY AT ANCHOR IN TOKYO BAY.

THE ALLIED REPRESENTATIVES WERE:

GENERAL OF THE ARMY DOUGLAS MACARTHUR,	THE SUPREME COMMANDER FOR THE ALLIED POWERS
FLEET ADMIRAL CHESTER W. NIMITZ,	UNITED STATES OF AMERICA
GENERAL HSU YUNG-CHANG,	REPUBLIC OF CHINA
ADMIRAL SIR BRUCE A. FRASER,	UNITED KINGDOM OF GREAT BRITAIN AND NORTHERN IRELAND
LIEUTENANT GENERAL KUZMA NIKOLAEVICH DEREVYANKO,	UNION OF SOVIET SOCIALISTIC REPUBLICS
GENERAL SIR THOMAS BLAMEY,	COMMONWEALTH OF AUSTRALIA
COLONEL L. MOORE COSGRAVE,	CANADA
GENERAL JACQUES LE CLERC,	REPUBLIC OF FRANCE
AIR VICE MARSHALL LEONARD M. ISITT,	DOMINION OF NEW ZEALAND
ADMIRAL C. E. L. HELFRICH,	KINGDOM OF THE NETHERLANDS

WITH THEIR STAFFS AND OBSERVING FLAG AND GENERAL OFFICERS.

THE JAPANESE REPRESENTATIVES WERE:

MAMORU SHIGEMITSU,	JAPANESE FOREIGN MINISTER
GENERAL YOSHIJIRO UMEZU,	CHIEF OF STAFF, JAPANESE ARMY HEADQUARTERS

WITH NINE STAFF AND OBSERVING OFFICERS.

AT 0904, THE JAPANESE REPRESENTATIVES SIGNED THE INSTRUMENT OF THEIR COUNTRY'S SURRENDER.

AT 0908, GENERAL OF THE ARMY DOUGLAS MACARTHUR, THE SUPREME COMMANDER FOR THE ALLIED POWERS, SIGNED FOR ALL THE NATIONS JOINED IN THE WAR AGAINST JAPAN. HE WAS ACCOMPANIED BY LIEUTENANT GENERAL JONATHAN M. WAINWRIGHT, THE COMMANDING GENERAL AT THE FALL OF CORREGIDOR IN 1942, AND BY LIEUTENANT GENERAL ARTHUR PERCIVAL, THE COMMANDING GENERAL AT THE FALL OF SINGAPORE IN THE SAME YEAR.

AT 0912, FLEET ADMIRAL CHESTER W. NIMITZ SIGNED FOR THE UNITED STATES. HE WAS ACCOMPANIED BY ADMIRAL WILLIAM F. HALSEY, COMMANDER OF THE UNITED STATES THIRD FLEET, AND BY REAR ADMIRAL FORREST P. SHERMAN, DEPUTY CHIEF OF STAFF TO ADMIRAL NIMITZ. REPRESENTATIVES OF THE OTHER ALLIED NATIONS THEN SIGNED. THIS COMPLETED THE CEREMONY OF SURRENDER.

SECOND MARKER on **MISSOURI'S** quarterdeck lists the names of Allied and Japanese principal actors in the drama of September 2, 1945.

INDEX

158

BIBLIOGRAPHY

These reference books proved particularly valuable in preparing the manuscript:

Victory in the Pacific 1945, Samuel Eliot Morison, Atlantic-Little, Brown, 1960

The Sea War in Korea, Malcolm W. Cagle & Frank A. Manson, U.S. Naval Institute, 1957

Pearl Harbor: Why, How, Fleet Salvage and Final Appraisal, Homer N. Wallin, Naval History Division, 1968

The Fall of Japan, William Craig, Dell Publishing Co., 1968

The United States Navy in World War II, S. E. Smith, William Morrow & Co., 1966

U.S. Navy at War, 1941-1945, Fleet Admrial Ernest J. King, U.S. Navy Department, 1946

All photographs not specifically credited otherwise are official U.S. Navy photographs.

Victory

at

Sea

. . . a selected album of photographs portraying the fighting career of U.S.S. *Missouri* and her contemporaries of the United States Navy in two wars.

—Official U.S. Navy photographs and courtesy of Admiral James S. Russell, USN (Ret.)

"CONTROL OF THE SEAS MEANS SECURITY; CONTROL OF THE SEAS MEANS PEACE; CONTROL OF THE SEA MEANS VICTORY."

—John F. Kennedy

GUNS OVER GOTHAM: With the New York skyline in the background, commissioning guests and ship's crew on the after main deck stand at attention as the Stars and Stripes are hoisted for the first time and the band plays the National Anthem.

CONDITION WATCH in Japanese waters.

MIGHTY MO ON MANEUVERS demonstrates her ability to make a tight turn.

BELOW THE WATERLINE, midshipmen stand watch at engine room control station.

FIRST THUNDER of the **MISSOURI'S** 16-inch guns during early gunnery practice following her commissioning provided this classic photograph. While burning gasses still belch from the forward gun muzzles and a jet of disturbed water spread below them, the six projectiles are caught in flight at the upper right.

KAMIKAZED! This photograph taken from U.S.S. **FRANKLIN,** which had just escaped a kamikaze bomb, shows the carrier **BELLEAU WOOD** after the same plane crashed her stern. A few months later the **FRANKLIN,** having ventured closer to Japan than any other Allied carrier, was struck by Japanese bombers while returning to Ulithi in company with the **MISSOURI.** She lay dead in the water 50 miles from the Japanese coast, listing 13 degrees, swept by flames and wracked by explosions. With 724 of her crew killed and 265 wounded, she returned to the United States for repair under her own power.

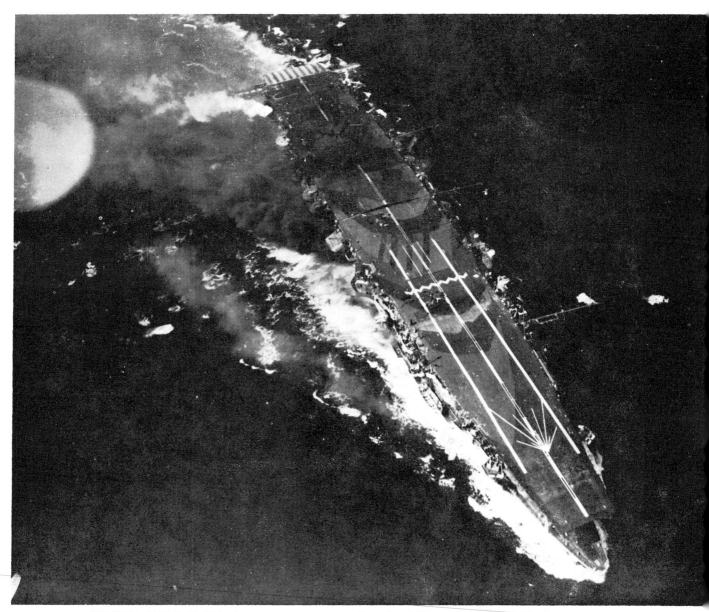

SCRATCH ONE FLAT TOP: Japanese carrier **ZUINO,** doomed and blazing, but still steaming fast, is pictured here in the final moments of her duel with Air Group 20 from U.S.S. **ENTERPRISE.**

The photo was taken from a torpedo plane seconds before its underwater missile struck the **ZUINO** on the starboard side, helping to sink her. The Imperial Japanese Navy, which opened hostilities with a heavy preponderance of aircraft carriers over the United States, found herself with none at all in the closing months of the war.

DIRECT HIT by a torpedo from an American fleet submarine
resulted in this spectacular demise of a Japanese gunboat which
got in the way of the Fast Carrier Force.

PERISCOPE PHOTO taken by Lieutenant Commander D. W. Morton, skipper of the submarine **WAHOO** during a war patrol, caught a Japanese transport making her final plunge. Seven other enemy ships fell victims to **WAHOO'S** deadly torpedoes during that cruise.

HUNTING THE HUNTER: Destroyers, deadly enemies of the submarines, weren't always winners. Above and at the right are periscope photographs from the **WAHOO** which portray with dramatic realism the sinking of a torpedoed Japanese destroyer. Those at the left show a large Japanese transport which suffered the same fate.

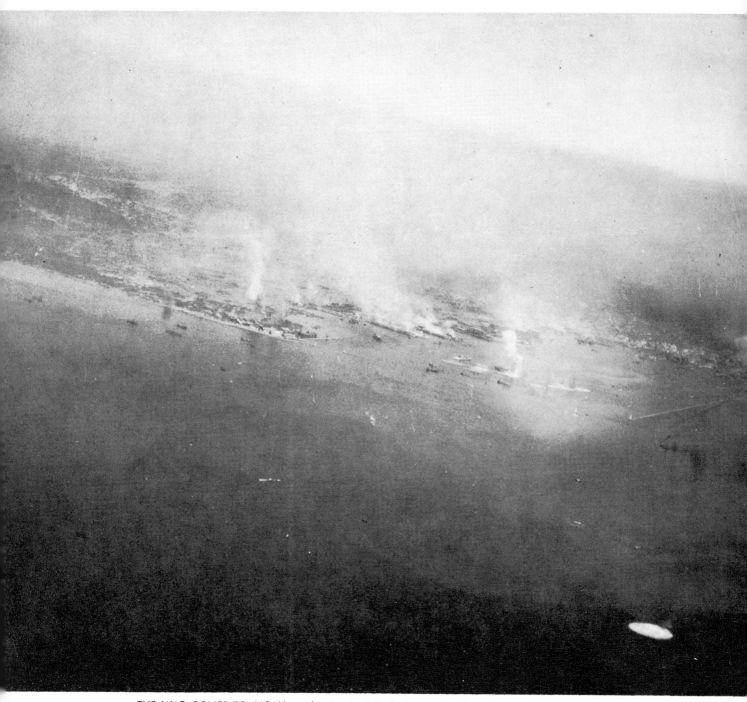

THE WAR COMES TO JAPAN, as shipping in Kobe harbor on Honshu Island is attacked March 19, 1945 by carrier planes of Task Group 58.2.

BOMBS AWAY! Izumi Airfield, Kyushu, under attack on March 18, 1945 by carrier planes of Rear Admiral Ralph Davison's Task Group 58.2.

THE WRATH OF THE FAST CARRIERS is unleashed on Tokyo, capital of the Imperial Japanese Empire, in the February raids of Task Force 58.

CHANGE OF FLAGS: Staff of Commander, Carrier Division 2 transferring from **FRANKLIN** to **ENTERPRISE,** the **FRANKLIN** having been ordered home for repairs.

MISSOURI at flank speed.

THE WAR IS OVER, and Admiral Nimitz signs the surrender document on the quarterdeck of the U.S.S. **MISSOURI,** September 2, 1945.

FOUR YEARS LATER, men of the **MISSOURI,** on Midshipmen Training Cruise, gather on the Surrender Deck to hear message from General of the Army Douglas MacArthur.

LADY IN TROUBLE: **MISSOURI** aground on Thimble Shoal, Chesapeake Bay, January 1950.

KOREAN COMBAT. Rocket ship and **MISSOURI'S** guns blast Red Chinese installations off Hungnam in December, 1950. Below, Seventh Fleet Commander Struble leaves his flagship **MISSOURI** to visit an advanced air base in Korea with General MacArthur.

Japanese plane exploding just ahead of the **MISSOURI** after being hit by anti-aircraft fire.

JAPANESE MIDGET SUBMARINE scores a torpedo hit on a tanker at Ulithi.

View from **MISSOURI'S** bow as one of the sixteen inch guns churns water with its blast.

PEARL HARBOR before the Japanese attack of December 7, 1941, above. U.S.S. **ARIZONA** is pictured in her death throes below; **TENNESSEE** and **WEST VIRGINIA** astern.

"LET HIM WHO KNOWS NOT HOW TO PRAY GO TO SEA"
. . . *John Ray, English Proverb*

THE CHURCH FLAG flies above the Stars and Stripes as men of the **MISSOURI** attend worship services on deck.

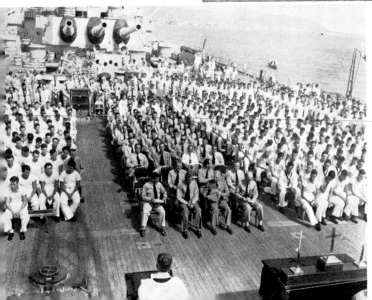

THE END